COPPER CHEF
GRILL & GRIDDLE

ERIC THEISS

First Edition

Published by Tristar Products, Inc.

Printed in China.

CCG_COOKBOOK_TP_ENG_V1_170515

Acknowledgments

This project involved several key people without whom it would not have been possible. I'd like to thank Claire Winslow for her endless testing and tweaking of recipes, and Lynda Gentile for driving tough deadlines in the nicest way. I want to thank Matt Wagemann for his fantastic photography. I'd also like to thank Kris "Chez" Amerine for his culinary wisdom and comedic contributions along the way, which always help to make a project more fun. As always, thank you to Meredith Laurence, "The Blue Jean Chef," who never tires of having my back whenever I need her. I am very grateful to Keith Mirchandani and Josef Lavi for giving me this great opportunity.

I want to thank my wife, Jesse, for keeping our "life" in order while I focused on this project (and Cameron and Max for making that nearly impossible) and my mom, Arlene, who raised me to appreciate good food and taught me to always cook with love.

Eric Theiss

Table of Contents

About the Author

Eric Theiss's culinary savoir-faire started in northern New Jersey as a child when his Italian mother, on a hunch, borrowed from the public library his first cookbook at age 6. His mother was right, and Eric began a life of culinary work. As a young adult, he continued to fuel his passion for food and fine dining. During his early twenties, his love of food and wine manifested itself in working long nights in NJ restaurants, including his favorite kitchen of all at The Culinary Renaissance, where acclaimed chef Frank Falcinelli[1] exposed Eric to a level of culinary passion that inspired Eric to strive. In 1997 he took a leap of faith and opened his own fine dining restaurant and bar called Meritage in West Chester, PA--one that enjoyed rave reviews from some prominent Philadelphia food critics. Here, his dream of owning and operating a fine dining establishment was fully realized.

A few years later, utilizing his inventive and creative flair, Eric moved on to the culinary broadcast world, working in product development for not only QVC's proprietary kitchenware lines but also for celebrity lines (Paula Deen, Emeril, Rocco, Rachel Ray) as well as his own personal line of cool kitchen tools and cookware, Walah!

Eric has been a popular regular TV Chef presenter for over 15 years on QVC's live shows for his own brands as well as a variety of well-known national kitchen brands. Beyond that, Eric owns and operates a company that brokers into QVC many new and innovative products. His most recent business venture, a successful new publishing company (also named Walah!), publishes cookbooks and pamphlets and distributes them nationwide.

Paramount to his career thus far, Eric currently hosts several successful, award-winning long-form infomercials such as the Power Pressure Cooker XL and the Copper Chef, each of which has sold millions of units. Eric wrote this cookbook to complement the Copper Grill infomercial and it provides many delicious Grill Pan recipes.

Eric currently resides near the live studios at QVC in PA along with his wife Jessica and his two sons, Cameron and Maxwell.

[1] Owner of NY Restaurants Frankies 457, Frankies Sputino, Prime Meats and Café Pedlar.

Questions & Answers

Q: Should I marinate my food before grilling it and for how long?

A: Marinating makes for much tastier grilling. Marinate for at least an hour, but it's no problem to leave in the refrigerator overnight. Be sure to take the food out of the marinade and let it drip almost completely off of the food before grilling. Too much liquid on the food will result in steam, and steam is the enemy of great grill marks. Always re-apply flavor at the end by adding BBQ sauce or fresh herbs and spices.

Q: Why are my meats coming off the Grill Pan too dry?

A: First, you may have over cooked it. Once you cook out the juices, the meat will be dry. The other problem could be that you aren't waiting a minimum of 10 minutes before cutting your meat. If you cut the meat too soon, all of the juices run out, leaving a dryer, tougher result. Also, instead of picking up the meat with a fork which pierces the meat, use a tong or a spatula to ensure that your juices stay inside the meat and don't end up on your cutting board.

Q: Can the Grill Pan be used under the broiler?

A: Yes, our Pan can be used in your oven under the broiler. Other grill pans that do not have high heat handles or coating that can handle heat above 500° F cannot be used under your broiler. Being able to use our Grill Pan under the broiler allows for top down cooking and is perfect for "finishing" large pieces of meat or even simply melting cheese.

Q: Can the Grill Pan be used on the BBQ grill?

A: Yes, thanks to our heavy gauge cast aluminum core and our high heat resistant CeramiTech coating, cooking on an open flame or BBQ is no problem. It's especially great on your outdoor BBQ for things like shrimp or asparagus or anything that may fall through your grill grates.

Q: What kind of food is stovetop grilling best for?

A: Stovetop grills were invented to allow for high heat searing of meat and fish (among other foods) inside the home. Our Grill Pan has an advantage of extremely raised grilling ridges. This is important to get those amazing grill marks that add flavor and visual flair. Also, veggies hold up very well to the grilling and it brings out their natural sugars. Since you are cooking quickly, the integrity of the nutrients are preserved. If you are cooking thicker pieces of protein, get a great sear and grill marks on both sides then put the Grill Pan into a preheated oven to finish. Remember, the handles will be hot!

Q: Will you still get grilled flavor?

A: Yes, the only difference is that you won't get the flavor of charcoal or wood. But the grill marks are real and definitely give you that grilled flavor.

Q: Can I cook with BBQ sauce?

A: The short answer is yes. What I recommend is that you rub your meat or fish with a flavorful dry rub in the first stages of cooking. Then, when it's almost finished, rub on your favorite BBQ sauce and cook for a few more minutes. If you start cooking with sugary sauces, they will burn before your food is cooking. Putting the BBQ sauce on at the end will give your food a really pretty sheen.

Q: How do you get those great grill marks?

A: In order to get great color on your grill marks you need to get the Grill Pan hot, about 500° F or more. You will know it's hot enough when you put your food on the Grill Pan and it makes a loud sizzle noise. If the noise is soft, lift off the food and wait another minute. Never put cold food on a cold Grill Pan if you want great color.

Why Copper Chef Grill?

Grilling has become one of America's favorite ways to cook food. Whether it's outside on the grill or inside on the stovetop, grilling food gives it a unique and characteristic flavor we all crave for our meats, fish and vegetables. What gives grilled food that special flavor? When you cook that hot on a grill pan, the ridges will impart a char to parts of the food while the other parts cook more slowly. This differential allows for a combination of flavors to be imparted at the same time to your taste buds. The nice thing about cooking on a grill pan (on the grill top or stove top) is that your food won't suffer the effects of flare-ups that can impart too much of a charred flavor. Beyond that, everyone enjoys the grill marks for added visual flare as well as texture on the plate.

I wrote this cookbook so that you can use it with other grill pans and outdoor grills. What I love about my state-of-the-art Copper Chef Grill Pan is that our ridges are up to 5 times higher than most and the thick cast aluminum is a superior heat conductor for super hot cooking. Not only that, we capped the Copper Chef Grill Pan with an innovative, Stainless Steel Induction Plate that helps to spread the heat evenly and quickly to all four corners. Add to that the CeramiTech coating which can withstand the high heat of the outdoor grill as well as making for easy clean up afterwards. And don't worry—it's completely PTFE and PFOA free and dishwasher safe. When you cook with the Copper Chef Grill Pan, you avoid cooking on a dirty grill and you also avoid losing veggies or seafood that normally would fall through the grate. With my Copper Chef Grill Pan, you can grill like a professional chef!

Why Copper Chef Griddle?

Whether it's perfectly crisp pancakes or a juicy, seared burger, griddle cooking is unmistakably delicious. But it doesn't have to be loaded with extra grease, either. We designed the Copper Chef Griddle Pan with best-selling CeramiTech coating to give you an effortless, non-stick cooking experience. No extra oil is needed! You get mouthwatering, evenly cooked meals that lift right off the Pan and don't require hours of messy cleanup afterwards.

Traditionally we think of crispy, griddle-cooked pancakes and eggs with perfectly golden hash browns. With the Copper Chef Griddle Pan, breakfast is only the beginning. The extra-large, non-stick surface means possibilities are endless. Plus, the Stainless Steel Induction Plate guarantees even heat distribution over the entire Griddle Pan. Your steaks sear perfectly and even delicate salmon stays tender without drying out. The best part? It's ideal for warm desserts, like my ooey-gooey French Toast Sundae. With the Copper Chef Griddle Pan, all of your restaurant-favorites are non-stick easy—right in your own kitchen.

Equivalent Chart

The charts below use standard U.S. Government guidelines. The charts offer equivalents for United States, metric, and Imperial (U.K.) measures. All conversions are approximate and most have been rounded up or down to the nearest whole number.[1]

Examples below:

1 teaspoon = 4.929 millimeters - rounded up to 5 millimeters

1 ounce = 28.349 grams - rounded to 28 grams

Dry/Weight Measurements

		Ounces
1/16 teaspoon	a dash	
1/8 teaspoon	a pinch or 6 drops	
1/4 teaspoon	15 drops	
1/2 teaspoon	30 drops	
1 teaspoon	1/3 tablespoon	1/6 ounce
3 teaspoons	1 tablespoon	1/2 ounce
1 tablespoon	3 teaspoons	1/2 ounce
2 tablespoons	1/8 cup	1 ounce
4 tablespoons	1/4 cup	2 ounces
5 tablespoons plus 1 teaspoon	1/3 cup	2.6 ounces
8 tablespoons	1/2 cup	4 ounces
10 tablespoons plus 2 teaspoons	2/3 cup	5.2 ounces
12 tablespoons	3/4 cup	6 ounces
16 tablespoons	1 cup	8 ounces
32 tablespoons	2 cups	16 ounces
64 tablespoons	4 cups or 1 quart	32 ounces

Liquid or Volume Measurements

	Pint	Quart	Gallon	U.S. Fluid Ounce	U.S. Tablespoon
jigger or measure	-	-	-	1.5	3
1 cup	1/2	-	-	8	16
2 cups	1	-	-	16	32
4 cups	2	1	1/4	32	64

[1] http://whatscookingamerica.net/Q-A/equiv.htm

Cooking Temperature Chart

Safe steps in food handling, cooking, and storage are essential in preventing foodborne illness. You can't see, smell, or taste harmful bacteria that may cause illness. In every step of food preparation, follow the four guidelines to help keep food safe:

Clean—Wash hands and surfaces often.

Separate—Separate raw meat from other foods.

Cook—Cook to the right temperature.

Chill—Refrigerate food promptly.

Cook all food to these minimum internal temperatures as measured with a food thermometer before removing food from the heat source. Let rest for a minimum of 10 minutes before serving, unless indicated otherwise.

Doneness	Eric's Recommended Serving Temperature	USDA Recommended Serving Temperature
Beef, Lamb, Pork, Veal Steaks, Chops & Roasts		
Rare	125° F (52° C)	*
Medium-rare	130° F (54° C)	*
Medium	135° F (57° C)	*Minimum Internal Temperature & Rest Time:
Medium-well	150° F (65° C)	145° F (63° C) and allow to rest for at least
Well-done	Over 150° F (over 65° C)	3 minutes
Ground Meats, Burgers, Meat Loaf & Sausages, Except Poultry		
Recommended	160° F (71° C)	*Minimum Internal Temperature: 160° F (71° C)
Burgers (Beef)		
Recommended	140° F (60° C)	160° F (71° C)
Pork Ribs, Pork Shoulders		
Tender and Juicy	180-190° F (82-88° C)	*
Pre-cooked Ham		
Recommended	140° F (60° C)	*Reheat cooked hams packaged in USDA-inspected plants to 140° F (60° C); all others to 165° F (74° C)
Turkey & Chicken, Whole or Ground		
Recommended	165° F (74° C)	*Minimum Internal Temperature: 165° F (74° C)
Fish		
Rare	125° F (52° C)	*
Medium	135° F (57° C)	*
Well-done	145° F (63° C)	*Minimum Internal Temperature: 145° F (63° C)
Unpasteurized Eggs		
Recommended	160° F (71° C)	*Minimum Internal Temperature: 160° F (71° C)

*Consuming raw or undercooked meats, poultry, seafood, shellfish, or eggs may increase your risk of foodborne illness.
*http://fsis.usda.gov/

Eric's Favorite Rubs

I like to make these rubs and store them in small **air-tight containers**. These recipes **yield about a ½ cup**. Making extra rubs saves time and money, and you will definitely enjoy having some versatile flavors at the ready in your cooking arsenal. Use these rubs not just for meat, fish and poultry; you can also sprinkle the Everyday Rub on a salad for some extra punch. Try the Poultry Rub on grilled veggies. The Red Meat Rub is great for flavoring your meatloaf mix. The idea is to play around and see how many different things you can do with them!

Poultry

2 tbsp. crushed sea salt

2 tbsp. paprika

1 tsp. sugar

1 tbsp. turmeric

2 tsp. garlic powder

2 tsp. granulated dried onion

1 tbsp. ground thyme

1 tsp. mustard powder

½ tsp. cayenne

2 tsp. dried lemon peel

1 tbsp. black ground pepper

Everyday

2 tbsp. crushed sea salt

2 tbsp. crushed black pepper

2 tbsp. granulated garlic

2 tbsp. granulated onion

1 tbsp. dried basil

½ tsp. red pepper flakes

1 tbsp. coriander

1 tsp. dry mustard

1 tsp. brown sugar

Fish

1 tbsp. crushed sea salt

1 tbsp. onion powder

1 tsp. thyme

2 tsp. tarragon

1 tbsp. dried parsley

1 tbsp. dried chives

1 tbsp. ground white pepper

1 tbsp. dried lemon peel

1 tsp. celery seed

Red Meat

2 tbsp. crushed sea salt

2 tbsp. brown sugar

2 tbsp. ground black coffee

1 tbsp. granulated garlic

1 tbsp. granulated onion

1 tbsp. cumin

1 tbsp. coriander

1 tbsp. ground black pepper

Directions: *Mix all of the ingredients together until well incorporated. You can make into a fine powder by placing into a blender or spice grinder.*

Appetizers

Grilled Stuffed Portobello Mushrooms

SERVES 2

Ingredients

2 large portobello mushrooms, with stems

2 tbsp. olive oil

1 clove garlic, peeled & minced

3 cups spinach

2 plum tomatoes, chopped

½ cup mozzarella, shredded

2 tbsp. Parmesan cheese, shredded

2 tbsp. panko breadcrumbs

½ cup bacon, cooked & chopped

Directions

1. Remove stems from portobello mushrooms and chop. Reserve caps whole.

2. In a sauté pan, cook garlic in olive oil for 3 minutes. Add spinach and mushroom stems. Cook until tender.

3. Arrange portobello caps on the Grill Pan. Fill with spinach mixture and tomatoes. Grill to desired doneness.

4. Preheat the broiler. Sprinkle both cheeses and breadcrumbs over stuffed mushrooms.

5. Cook portobellos under the broiler until breadcrumbs are toasted to desired doneness.

6. Top with crisp bacon before serving.

Eric's Tip: I love to turn these into an Eggs Benedict-style dish by topping with a poached egg.

Cheese-Stuffed Dates

Ingredients

¼ cup bleu cheese

¼ cup cream cheese

20 dates

10 slices bacon, raw, cut in half

Directions

1. Preheat the oven to 400° F.

2. Mix the cheeses together. Set aside.

3. Make a slit, lengthwise, into each date. Stuff with cheese mixture.

4. Roll each date with bacon. Grill 2-3 minutes on each side.

5. Cook in the oven for 8-10 minutes or until bacon is crispy.

Eric's Tip: I'll add a shelled pistachio or walnut into each date for an extra crunch.

Korean Beef Skewers

SERVES 10

Ingredients

1 lb. beef flank steak, cut into strips

Marinade

½ cup soy sauce

1 tbsp. rice vinegar

¼ cup brown sugar

2 tbsp. sesame oil

2 cloves garlic, peeled & minced

4 scallions, sliced

To Serve

1 tsp. sesame seeds

1 tsp. crushed red pepper

Directions

1. Combine steak with marinade ingredients in the refrigerator for 2 hours.

2. Skewer steak strips. Preheat the Grill Pan on medium heat for 5 minutes.

3. Grill beef skewers on each side to desired doneness.

4. Sprinkle with sesame seeds and crushed red pepper before serving.

Eric's Tip: Serve with some jasmine rice and bibb lettuce for delicious wraps.

Chicken Satay

Ingredients

Peanut Sauce

1 cup peanut butter

2 tbsp. shallots, minced

2 tbsp. brown sugar

½ tsp. curry

1 tbsp. soy sauce

1 tbsp. mirin rice wine

1 lime, juiced

1 clove garlic, peeled & minced

———————

2 chicken breasts, sliced thin

Garnish

½ cup peanuts, chopped

scallions, chopped

Directions

1. Peanut sauce: combine peanut butter, shallots, brown sugar, curry, soy sauce, mirin, lime juice, and garlic. Mix.

2. Marinate chicken in peanut sauce for 4 hours in the refrigerator.

3. Preheat the Grill Pan on medium heat for 5 minutes.

4. Skewer the chicken. Grill on both sides until done.

5. Top skewers with chopped peanuts and scallions before serving.

Eric's Tip: I love to substitute the chicken for shrimp then toss them with chilled sesame noodles.

Mozzarella Crostini & Grilled Tomatoes

SERVES 6

Ingredients

Olive Oil Marinade

½ cup extra virgin olive oil

2 cloves garlic, peeled & minced

1 tsp. dried oregano

½ tsp. sea salt

½ tsp. ground black pepper

½ crusty baguette, sliced into ½ inch rounds

1 cup grape tomatoes

12 slices fresh mozzarella

2 tbsp. balsamic glaze

3 basil leaves, chopped, for garnish

Directions

1. Marinade: in a bowl, combine olive oil, garlic, oregano, sea salt, and pepper.

2. Brush the bread on both sides with some of the olive oil marinade. Grill on both sides to desired doneness.

3. Toss the tomatoes with remaining marinade. Grill to desired doneness.

4. Assemble crostini: arrange mozzarella on top of each slice of bread. Top with tomatoes.

5. Drizzle balsamic glaze and any leftover olive oil marinade over crostini. Garnish with basil immediately before serving.

Eric's Tip: If you can't find nice ripe tomatoes, grill some zucchini and top with chopped sun-dried tomato.

Grilled Peach & Pineapple Salsa

SERVES 4

Ingredients

2 peaches, pitted

1 cup pineapple, sliced

½ red onion, sliced in rings

½ red pepper, sliced

2 tbsp. cilantro, chopped

1 tbsp. lime juice

½ jalapeño

1 tsp. sugar

½ tsp. sea salt

blue corn tortilla chips, to serve

Directions

1. Grill fruit and vegetables whole on all sides before chopping.

2. Dice the fruits and vegetables. Toss with cilantro, lime juice, jalapeño, sugar, and sea salt.

3. Serve grilled fruit with chips.

Eric's Tip: If there is any left over, I like to add it to my Jasmine rice for a delicious island-style side dish.

27

Mushroom Bruschetta

Ingredients

Baguette

1 baguette, split

¼ cup extra virgin olive oil

2 cloves garlic, peeled

8 slices mozzarella cheese

Mushrooms

6 portobello mushrooms

¼ cup olive oil

2 sprigs rosemary, chopped

1 tsp. sea salt

To Serve

1 tbsp. balsamic glaze

1 tbsp. chopped parsley

Directions

1. Brush the baguette with extra virgin olive oil. Grill to desired doneness. Rub with the garlic clove for flavor.

2. Top with mozzarella and set aside.

3. Toss the portobello mushrooms with olive oil, rosemary, and sea salt. Grill to desired doneness. Slice and layer on top of the mozzarella.

4. Immediately before serving, drizzle bruschetta with balsamic glaze and sprinkle with parsley.

Eric's Tip: Cremini mushrooms are just baby portobellos so you can swap them out if you wish.

Cheese-Stuffed Sweet Mini Peppers

Ingredients

8 oz. cream cheese, softened

½ cup pepperoni, chopped

⅔ cup Asiago cheese

⅔ cup mozzarella cheese

2 tbsp. basil, chopped

12 mini peppers, cut in half & seeded

scallions, for garnish

Directions

1. In a bowl, combine cream cheese, pepperoni, Asiago, mozzarella and basil. Mix.

2. Stuff the peppers with the cream cheese filling.

3. Preheat the oven to 400° F.

4. Grill the peppers on medium heat until tender.

5. Place the Grill Pan in the oven for 5-10 minutes until peppers are cooked through. Sprinkle with scallions before serving.

Eric's Tip: Wrap the peppers in bacon for awesome poppers!

Maryland Crab Cakes

SERVES 4

Ingredients

1 lb. crabmeat, lump

1 egg

¾ cup soda crackers, crushed

1 tbsp. Dijon mustard

1 tsp. seafood seasoning

1 shallot, peeled & minced

¼ cup mayonnaise

½ tsp. ground black pepper

1 red pepper, small dice

2 tbsp. canola oil

To Serve

tartar sauce

lemon wedges

Directions

1. Mix all the ingredients together except the oil.

2. Form into four 3 oz. cakes.

3. Pour the oil onto the Griddle Pan. On medium heat, cook crab cakes on both sides until golden.

4. Serve with tartar sauce and lemon wedges.

Griddle Recipe

Eggs in a Basket

Ingredients

4 slices white bread

¼ cup margarine

4 eggs

½ cup shredded cheddar cheese

salt

pepper

Directions

1. Butter the bread on one side.

2. Cut a hole into the center of the bread.

3. Preheat the Griddle Pan on medium heat for 3-4 minutes.

4. Arrange bread, buttered side down, onto the Griddle Pan.
    Crack an egg into the center of each slice. Sprinkle with cheddar cheese.

5. Cook on both sides, about 3-4 minutes.

6. Season with salt and pepper before serving.

Griddle Recipe

Chive Avocado Goat Cheese Omelet

SERVES 1

Ingredients

3 egg whites, beaten

1 tbsp. chopped chives

¼ tsp. sea salt

¼ tsp. ground black pepper

1 tbsp. grape seed oil

2 tbsp. goat cheese, crumbled

½ avocado, sliced

Directions

1. Combine egg whites with chives, salt, and pepper in a bowl.

2. Pour the oil onto the Griddle Pan. Add egg whites.

3. Sprinkle goat cheese and avocado over the egg.

4. Cook to desired doneness. Fold omelet before plating and serving.

Griddle Recipe

Salads

Grilled Chicken & Pineapple Salad

SERVES 2

Ingredients

Marinade

3 tbsp. olive oil

1 tsp. sea salt

½ tsp. ground black pepper

½ tsp. onion powder

½ tsp. garlic powder

½ tsp. paprika

2 tbsp. red wine vinegar

¼ pineapple, trimmed & cut into wedges

2 chicken breasts

Dressing

juice of ½ lemon

¼ cup extra virgin olive oil

½ tsp. sea salt

½ tsp. ground black pepper

1 tsp. honey

---

3 cups kale

1 cup quinoa, cooked

Directions

1. In a bowl, combine marinade ingredients. Marinate chicken in the refrigerator for 1 hour.

2. Grill the pineapple on both sides until tender.

3. Grill the chicken 6-7 minutes on each side until cooked.

4. Dressing: in a bowl, combine lemon juice, extra virgin olive oil, sea salt, pepper, and honey.

5. Toss kale and quinoa with dressing. Top with grilled pineapple.

6. Allow chicken to rest before slicing and serving with salad.

Eric's Tip: I love to add feta cheese then roll it up in a tortilla for a killer burrito!

Grilled Chipotle Chicken Salad

Ingredients

Marinade

2 chipotle peppers

1 clove garlic, peeled & minced

½ tsp. sea salt

½ tsp. ground coriander

2 tbsp. olive oil

½ lime, juiced

2 chicken breasts

Dressing

¼ cup buttermilk

1 tbsp. Worcestershire sauce

½ tsp. garlic powder

½ tsp. onion powder

½ tsp. sea salt

½ tsp. ground black pepper

½ tsp. Dijon mustard

1 tsp. sugar

Salad

4 cups romaine, chopped

½ cup grape tomatoes, halved

½ red onion, peeled & sliced

½ cucumber, sliced

Directions

1. Combine all marinade ingredients in a bowl. Marinate chicken in the refrigerator for 1 hour.

2. Combine all dressing ingredients in a bowl. Set aside.

3. Grill chicken on medium heat 5-7 minutes per side or until chicken is fully cooked.

4. In a large bowl, toss salad ingredients with dressing.

5. Let chicken rest before slicing and serving over the salad.

Eric's Tip: I love to get pre-made pizza dough, roll it thin, then grill it for the best salad pizza.

Ingredients

Caesar Dressing

1 lemon, juiced

½ cup olive oil

2 egg yolks

6 anchovies

1 clove garlic, peeled

1 tbsp. mustard

½ tsp. Worcestershire sauce

salt & pepper to taste

Croutons

1 cup cubed baguette

½ tbsp. garlic powder

½ tsp. sea salt

2 tbsp. olive oil

Shrimp Marinade

2 tbsp. olive oil

1 tsp. sea salt

1 tsp. black pepper, ground

1 tbsp. lemon juice

---

12 shrimp, extra large (16-20 size), peeled & deveined

To Serve

1 head romaine, chopped

¼ cup Parmesan cheese, grated

Grilled Shrimp Caesar Salad

Directions

1. Caesar dressing: combine egg yolks, anchovies, garlic, and 1 tbsp. lemon juice in a food processor. Very slowly, drizzle in half of the olive oil (¼ cup). Add remaining olive oil and lemon juice, mustard, and Worcestershire sauce. Season with salt and pepper, to taste.

2. Croutons: in a bowl, toss the cubed bread with garlic powder, sea salt, and olive oil. Grill croutons on all sides on medium heat.

3. Shrimp marinade: in a bowl, combine olive oil, sea salt, black pepper, and lemon juice.

4. Toss shrimp in marinade. Grill on each side until done.

5. In a bowl, combine romaine, croutons, and ½ cup Caesar dressing. Toss gently.

6. Divide the salad between two plates. Top with six shrimp each. Sprinkle with Parmesan cheese before serving.

Eric's Tip: Salmon or tuna fillets work well with this dish too!

Warm Tomato Caprese

Ingredients

1 eggplant, sliced ¼ in. thick

¼ cup extra virgin olive oil

1 tsp. sea salt

½ tsp black pepper, ground

1 clove garlic, peeled & minced

1 lb. mozzarella, sliced

3 beefsteak tomatoes,
slice ½ in. thick

To Serve

2 tbsp. extra virgin olive oil

1 tbsp. balsamic glaze

1 tbsp. basil pesto

2 tbsp. pea tendrils

Directions

1. In a bowl, combine eggplant, ¼ cup extra virgin olive oil, salt, pepper, and garlic. Mix.

2. Grill the eggplant on each side until tender.

3. Assemble caprese: layer eggplant, mozzarella, and tomato on a plate.

4. Drizzle with extra virgin olive oil and balsamic glaze. Repeat to make three more caprese towers.

5. Drizzle with basil pesto and pea tendrils before serving.

Eric's Tip: Turn this into a party appetizer by shingling the tomato and grilled eggplant around burrata mozzarella.

Grilled Scallops with Green Goddess Dressing

SERVES 3

Ingredients

Green Goddess Dressing

3 anchovies

3 tbsp. chives

¾ cup parsley

¼ cup tarragon

1 clove garlic, peeled

1 cup mayonnaise

1 cup sour cream

2 tbsp. lemon juice

1 tsp. sea salt

½ tsp. black pepper, ground

Scallop Marinade

¼ cup olive oil

½ tsp. sea salt

½ tbsp. black pepper, ground

1 lb. scallops, large

2 cups baby arugula

Directions

1. In a blender, combine all dressing ingredients until smooth.

2. Marinate scallops: in a separate bowl, combine scallops, olive oil, sea salt, and pepper.

3. Grill the scallops on each side on medium heat until done.

4. Divide the arugula onto three plates. Arrange scallops on top. Spoon dressing onto each salad before serving.

Eric's Tip: I like to add the leftovers the next day with some cooked pasta for a delicious salad.

Grilled Watermelon Salad

SERVES 2

Ingredients

1 (2-in. thick) slice watermelon, with rind

1 cup micro greens

1 tbsp. extra virgin olive oil

1 tsp. lemon juice

sea salt & pepper

1 cup feta cheese

1 small red onion, sliced thin

1 cup strawberries, sliced

⅓ cup pine nuts. toasted

Directions

1. Grill watermelon on both sides.

2. In a bowl, toss micro greens with olive oil, lemon juice, sea salt, and pepper.

3. Sprinkle watermelon with feta, red onion, strawberries, and pine nuts.

4. Top with micro greens. Cut into slices before serving.

Eric's Tip: You can very easily turn this salad into an entrée by adding grilled chicken or shrimp, but my personal favorite is adding some thin sliced prosciutto.

Grilled Corn Salad

SERVES 4

Ingredients

6 cobs corn, grilled, corn removed

½ red onion, diced

½ cup celery, diced

½ cup red bell peppers, diced

2 tbsp. cilantro

1 clove fresh garlic, chopped

juice of ½ lime

¼ cup extra virgin olive oil

½ tsp. sea salt

½ tsp. ground black pepper

¼ cup sour cream, to garnish

Directions

1. In a bowl, combine all ingredients except sour cream.

2. Serve corn salad topped with sour cream. It's an extremely versatile side dish that's delicious with chicken, meat, and fish.

Eric's Tip: Another variation on this is to whiz it a few times with a hand blender or food processor, then substitute the sour cream for mayonnaise to make an interesting aioli. You can use it as a delicious sandwich spread or as a base for chicken salad.

Arugula Salad & Grilled Tomato Vinaigrette

SERVES 4

Ingredients

12 slices bacon

2 pears, cored & cut in half

Tomato Vinaigrette

6 plum tomatoes, cut in half

½ cup extra virgin olive oil

1 tsp. sea salt

½ tsp. ground black pepper

3 cloves garlic, peeled & sliced

3 tbsp. red wine vinegar

6 cups baby arugula

½ cup crumbled bleu cheese

⅓ cup pumpkin seeds, toasted

Directions

1. Grill bacon until crispy. Set aside.

2. Grill pears in remaining bacon fat.

3. Vinaigrette: in a bowl, combine tomatoes, olive oil, sea salt, pepper, and garlic. Reserve vinegar for later.

4. Remove tomatoes and garlic from vinaigrette. Grill to desired doneness. Return garlic to vinaigrette.

5. Once cool, chop tomatoes and return to the vinaigrette. Add vinegar and mix gently.

6. In a separate bowl, toss arugula with vinaigrette, bleu cheese, and pumpkins seeds.

7. Divide salad onto 4 plates. Top each with three slices bacon and half a pear before serving.

Eric's Tip: A grilled salmon or chicken breast turns this salad into the main course.

Grilled Bread Salad

SERVES 4-6

Ingredients

Vinaigrette

½ cup extra virgin olive oil

¼ cup red wine vinegar

1 clove garlic, peeled & minced

salt and pepper

---

1 French baguette,
sliced 1-inch thick

1 lb. large cherry tomatoes,
quartered

2 cucumbers, quartered & cut into
1-inch medallions

1 medium red onion,
halved & sliced

¼ cup fresh basil, chopped

Directions

1. In a bowl, combine the olive oil, vinegar, and garlic. Mix. Season with salt and pepper.

2. Grill the bread on both sides. Cut into quarters.

3. Toss grilled bread with vinaigrette and remaining ingredients immediately before serving.

Eric's Tip: Drizzle some romaine hearts with salt, pepper and olive oil. Then grill for a few minutes to get a nice char.

Sandwiches

Grilled Shrimp Po'Boy

Cheddar Jalapeño Stuffed Burger

Buffalo Chicken Burger

Skirt Steak
& Tomato Tapenade Sandwich

Lamb & Goat Cheese Burger

Kimchi Korean Burger

Mac & Cheese Panini

Caramelized Mushroom Panini

Mozzarella & Pepperoncini
Stuffed Burger

Italian Panini

Philly Cheesesteak

Patty Melt

Chicken Broccoli Rabe Panini

Grilled Shrimp Po'Boy

SERVES 4

Ingredients

1 lb. shrimp, 21-25 size.

Marinade

2 tbsp. olive oil

1 lemon, juiced

2 cloves garlic, peeled & minced

1 tsp. paprika

½ tsp. cumin

Remoulade

¼ cup mayonnaise

¼ cup Russian dressing

1 pinch seafood seasoning

1 pinch cayenne pepper

2 cups shredded lettuce

2 tomatoes, sliced

4 hoagie rolls

Directions

1. Combine shrimp with marinade ingredients. Grill on both sides until done.

2. In a bowl, mix together remoulade ingredients.

3. Arrange lettuce and tomato slices onto each roll. Add shrimp. Top with remoulade sauce before serving.

Eric's Tip: The versatility of the Po'Boy Sandwich is endless. You can swap out the shrimp for any number of things. Grilled chicken, burgers, blackened catfish, pulled pork. . . they have it all in New Orleans!

Cheddar Jalapeño Stuffed Burger

SERVES 4

Ingredients

Burger Mixture

2 lb. ground beef

1 tsp. sea salt

1 tsp. ground black pepper

3 tbsp. cilantro, chopped

½ small onion, peeled & minced

1 jalapeño, seeded & chopped

---

4 ½ oz. cheddar cheese,
cut into chunks

2 tbsp. olive oil

4 slices cheddar cheese

4 brioche rolls

¼ cup margarine

16 pickled jalapeño rings

Directions

1. Combine ground beef, sea salt, pepper, cilantro, onion, and jalapeño.

2. Divide ground beef mixture into 4 balls. Stuff each ball with a chunk of cheddar.

3. Rub burgers with olive oil. Grill about 5 minutes per side or to desired doneness.

4. Top burgers with sliced cheddar.

5. Spread each roll with margarine. Grill to desired doneness. Serve burgers topped with pickled jalapeños.

Eric's Tip: If you have fresh sliced jalapeños, heat 1 cup vinegar and ¼ cup sugar, then pour over the peppers and let sit for 30 minutes for a quick pickle.

Buffalo Chicken Burger

SERVES 4

Ingredients

Burger Mixture

2 lb. ground chicken

1 tsp. sea salt

1 tsp. ground black pepper

1 cup bleu cheese

3 tbsp. ranch dressing

2 tbsp. melted butter

¼ cup hot pepper sauce

---

2 tbsp. olive oil

¼ cup margarine

4 brioche rolls

4 lettuce leaves

4 slices tomato

4 slices red onion

Directions

1. In a bowl, combine ground chicken, sea salt, black pepper, bleu cheese, ranch, melted butter, and hot pepper sauce. Form into 4 balls.

2. Rub burgers with olive oil. Grill on medium heat 5-7 minutes per side or until fully cooked.

3. Spread margarine on one side of each roll. Grill to desired doneness.

4. Arrange burgers on brioche rolls. Top with lettuce, tomato, and red onion before serving with your favorite side dishes.

Eric's Tip: You can use any kind of ground meat with amazing results. Just adjust your cooking time accordingly.

Skirt Steak & Tomato Tapenade Sandwich

SERVES 3

Ingredients

1 lb. skirt steak

1 shallot, peeled & minced

3 tbsp. balsamic vinegar

¼ cup olive oil

½ tsp. sea salt

½ tsp. course ground black pepper

3 slices focaccia, grilled

Tomato Red Onion Tapenade

¼ cup olive oil

2 tbsp. red wine vinegar

1 clove garlic, peeled & minced

½ tsp. sea salt

¼ tsp. ground black pepper

3 roma tomatoes, chopped

¼ red onion, diced

6 basil leaves, chopped

Directions

1. In a shallow pan, marinate steak with shallots, balsamic vinegar, olive oil, sea salt, and pepper for 1 hour.

2. Combine tapenade ingredients in a bowl. Set aside.

3. Grill the steak to desired temperature. Let rest 10 minutes before slicing.

4. Assemble sliced steak and tapenade open-face on focaccia. Serve with your favorite side dish.

Eric's Tip: Don't forget to let your steak rest for 5-10 minutes so it stays juicy. It's also important to slice the meat against the grain. For an extra special treat, add a little crumbled Gorgonzola cheese, I promise you won't be disappointed!

Lamb & Goat Cheese Burger

SERVES 3

Ingredients

1 lb. ground lamb

½ onion, peeled & minced

2 sprigs rosemary, chopped

1 clove garlic, peeled & minced

2 tbsp. olive oil

1 tsp. sea salt

1 tsp. black pepper ground

4 oz. goat cheese, crumbled

3 brioche hamburger rolls

2 tbsp. margarine

Directions

1. In a bowl, combine ground lamb, onion, rosemary, and garlic. Form into three patties.

2. Brush each burger with olive oil. Season with sea salt and pepper.

3. Grill to desired temperature. Top with goat cheese.

4. Spread margarine over each roll. Grill to desired doneness.

5. Arrange burgers onto the rolls. Serve with your favorite side dish.

Eric's Tip: If lamb is not available or just not to your liking, you can substitute any ground meat for this recipe. I've even ground up fresh fish in my food processor and made salmon sliders!

Kimchi Korean Burger

Ingredients

2 lb. ground beef

2 tbsp. soy sauce

2 tbsp. brown sugar

½ cup scallion, chopped

2 cloves garlic, peeled & minced

2 tbsp. sesame oil

2 tbsp. toasted sesame seeds

5 hamburger rolls

½ cup margarine

1 cup kimchi, diced

Directions

1. Combine ground beef with soy sauce, brown sugar, scallions, garlic, sesame oil, and sesame seeds. Form into five patties.

2. Spread margarine over each roll. Grill to desired doneness.

3. Grill burgers to desired temperature.

4. Arrange burgers onto the rolls. Top with kimchi. Serve with your favorite side dish.

Eric's Tip: A lot of times you will see an egg garnish in traditional Korean cuisine. I can't think of anything better to top this burger than a nice farm-fresh egg served sunny side up!

Mac & Cheese Panini

SERVES 4

Ingredients

2 cups heavy cream

½ tsp. sea salt

½ tsp. ground black pepper

2 tbsp. butter

1 tbsp. cornstarch

2 cups shredded cheddar

2 cups macaroni elbows, cooked

½ cup margarine

8 slices bread

16 slices American cheese, yellow

Directions

1. In a saucepan, bring the cream, sea salt, pepper & butter to a boil.

2. In a bowl, mix together cornstarch and shredded cheddar.

3. Add the cheddar mixture to the boiling cream. Whisk until creamy.

4. Combine macaroni with cheese sauce. Turn off heat and stir.

5. Butter each slice of bread with margarine on one side.

6. Assemble paninis on the Grill Pan buttered side down: 1 slice bread, 2 slices cheese, about ¾ cup mac and cheese, 2 more slices cheese, and 1 slice bread.

7. Grill on medium heat to desired doneness. Serve with your favorite soup or side dish.

Eric's Tip: I love to mix in 1 cup of crispy crumbled bacon into the mac and cheese, then add a few tomato slices onto the sandwich.

Caramelized Mushroom Panini

**MAKES 4
SANDWICHES**

Ingredients

1 lb. button mushrooms, sliced

¼ cup extra virgin olive oil

2 tsp. fresh thyme leaves

3 medium red onions,
peeled & sliced

½ cup red wine

¼ cup beef broth

salt and pepper

8 slices sourdough bread

½ cup margarine

16 slices Swiss cheese

Directions

1. In a frying pan, sauté mushrooms in 1 tbsp. olive oil until slightly tender. Add thyme and cook for an additional minute. Transfer to a bowl and set aside.

2. Sauté onions in the remaining olive oil until tender, about 10 minutes. Add red wine and cook until fully absorbed.

3. Pour in beef broth and cook until fully absorbed. Season with salt and pepper, to taste.

4. Brush one side of each slice of bread with margarine.

5. Set the Grill Pan on medium heat. Arrange 4 slices of bread on top, margarine side down.

6. Top each with 2 slices cheese, onions, mushrooms, 2 more slices cheese, and remaining slice of bread.

7. Grill paninis on each side until golden.

8. Serve warm with your favorite soup or side dishes.

Eric's Tip: The more variety the better. I love using a mix of mushrooms like shiitake, cremini and oyster mushrooms. Each has its own flavor and texture.

Mozzarella & Pepperoncini Stuffed Burger

SERVES 4

Ingredients

Burger Mixture

2 lb. ground beef

½ cup pepperoni, diced

1 tsp. sea salt

1 tsp. ground black pepper

1 tsp. garlic powder

1 tsp. onion powder

2 tbsp. BBQ sauce

---

4 slices fresh mozzarella

2 tbsp. olive oil

4 brioche rolls

¼ cup margarine

1 cup pepperoncini, for serving

Directions

1. Combine ground beef, pepperoni, sea salt, pepper, garlic and onion powders, and BBQ sauce.

2. Divide burger mixture into 4 balls. Stuff each with a slice of mozzarella.

3. Rub the burgers with olive oil. Grill on medium heat to desired doneness.

4. Butter brioche rolls with margarine. Grill to desired doneness.

5. Arrange stuffed burgers on brioche rolls. Serve with pepperoncini.

Eric's Tip: I love using a meatloaf mix of pork/beef/veal instead of the straight ground beef. It's available now at most markets.

Grill Press
Accessory is required for this recipe.

SERVES 2

Italian Panini

Ingredients

2 hoagie rolls, sliced in half lengthwise

¼ cup margarine

½ cup baby spinach

8 slices tomatoes, thin

¼ lb. pepperoni, sliced

¼ lb. salami, sliced

¼ ham, sliced

¼ lb. provolone cheese, sliced

¼ cup hot cherry peppers

Olive Oil Dressing

¼ cup olive oil

2 tbsp. red wine vinegar

1 tsp. dried oregano

½ tsp. sea salt

½ tsp. ground black pepper

Directions

1. Spread margarine on both halves of each roll. Arrange bottom halves onto the Grill Pan.

2. Top with spinach, tomatoes, pepperoni, salami, ham, provolone cheese, and cherry peppers.

3. In a shaker bottle, combine olive oil, vinegar, oregano, sea salt, and pepper. Shake. Distribute dressing onto the inside of the roll.

4. Finish with top halves of the roll. On medium heat, use the **Grill Press** to cook paninis on both sides to desired doneness.

5. Serve with your favorite potato chips.

Eric's Tip: If you are really in the mood for something extra special, substitute the ham, pepperoni and salami for a quality mortadella.

69

Philly Cheesesteak

SERVES 2

Ingredients

1 large white onion, halved, sliced

1 tbsp. canola oil

½ pound rib eye, sliced very thin

4 slices American cheese

kosher salt & freshly ground black pepper

2 hoagie rolls

Directions

1. Preheat the Griddle Pan over medium heat.

2. Add the onions and a splash of the canola oil to the center of the Pan.

3. Sauté, tossing often, until onions begin to caramelize. Push to one side of the Pan.

4. Add the rib eye. Cook, tossing often, until cooked through, about 3 minutes. Push to one side of the Pan.

5. Place 2 slices of American cheese in the center of the Pan. Top with half of the onions and half of the rib eye.

6. Repeat with remaining ingredients. Season with salt and pepper, to taste. Serve on hoagie rolls.

Griddle Recipe

Grill Press
Accessory is required for this recipe.

SERVES 2

Patty Melt

Ingredients

2 hamburgers, 6 oz. ea.

½ tsp. sea salt

½ tsp. ground black pepper

¼ cup margarine

4 slices rye bread

8 slices Swiss cheese

1 onion, sautéed

Directions

1. Preheat the Griddle Pan on high heat.

2. Rub the burgers with salt and pepper.

3. Cook the burgers to desired temperature.

4. Remove and set aside.

5. Wipe the Pan clean. Preheat on medium heat.

6. Butter the rye bread on one side.

7. Assemble the sandwiches: arrange two slices of rye onto the Pan. Top each with two slices cheese, onions, a burger, two more slices cheese, and a second slice of rye.

8. Place the **Grill Press** on the sandwiches. Cook until golden on each side.

9. Cut sandwiches before serving.

Griddle Recipe

Grill Press
Accessory is required for this recipe.

SERVES 2

Chicken Broccoli Rabe Panini

Ingredients

2 cloves garlic, thinly sliced

3 tbsp. extra virgin olive oil

½ bunch broccoli rabe, blanched

½ tsp. sea salt

¼ tsp. red pepper flakes

8 slices fresh mozzarella

2 chicken breasts, cooked

2 ciabatta rolls, cut

Directions

1. In a sauté pan, cook garlic in olive oil. Add broccoli rabe and cook until tender. Season with salt and red pepper flakes.

2. Preheat the Griddle Pan on medium heat.

3. Assemble the paninis: layer the broccoli rabe, mozzarella, and chicken onto the bottom half of each roll. Drizzle with the oil from the pan.

4. Top each sandwich with a second roll. Arrange onto the Pan with the **Grill Press** on top.

5. Cook on each side until golden.

6. Cut paninis before serving.

Griddle Recipe

Quesadillas

Teriyaki Chicken Quesadilla

Ingredients

Marinade

2 tbsp. teriyaki sauce

1 tbsp. orange juice concentrate

2 scallions, chopped

1 clove garlic, minced

½ tsp. red pepper flakes

1 tsp. ginger, minced

1 tsp. sesame oil

---

1 chicken breast, sliced in half

2 (8-in.) tortillas

¾ cup jack cheese, shredded

2 scallions, diced

3 tbsp. red pepper, diced

1 tsp. jalapeño, chopped

To Serve

2 tbsp. salsa

2 tbsp. sour cream

¼ cup guacamole

Directions

1. In a bowl, combine the marinade ingredients. Marinate chicken in the refrigerator for one hour.

2. Grill the chicken until cooked. Remove and dice.

3. Arrange tortilla on the Grill Pan. Layer with cheese, chicken, scallions, red peppers, and jalapeño. Top with the second tortilla.

4. Grill on both sides until cheese is melted.

5. Cut quesadilla into sections. Serve with salsa, sour cream, and guacamole.

Eric's Tip: You can go vegetarian by replacing the chicken with firm tofu. Slice the tofu in 1 inch slices, then press between two plates lined with paper towels for 15 minutes. After the excess moisture is drained, follow marinating and grilling instructions.

Mac & Cheese Quesadilla

SERVES 2

Ingredients

2 cups heavy cream

2 cups cheddar, shredded

1 tbsp. cornstarch

2 tbsp. butter

2 cups elbow macaroni, cooked

4 (8-in.) tortillas

12 slices American cheese, yellow

½ tsp. sea salt

½ tsp. ground black pepper

Directions

1. In a pot, bring heavy cream to a boil.

2. Combine cheddar and cornstarch in a bowl.

3. Add butter and cheddar cheese mixture to the hot cream. Stir until creamy.

4. Stir in macaroni until well incorporated. Set aside to cool.

5. Arrange 1 tortilla on the Grill Pan. Top with 3 slices American cheese, 1 cup mac and cheese, and 3 more slices American cheese. Season with salt and pepper. Complete with a second tortilla.

6. Grill quesadilla until cheese is melted and tortilla is cooked.

7. Repeat to make the second quesadilla.

Eric's Tip: My absolute favorite variation on this recipe is to give a good sprinkle of seafood seasoning, plus some sweet corn and fresh crab meat for a Maryland style quesadilla.

Turkey & Cranberry Quesadilla

SERVES 1

Ingredients

2 (8-in.) tortillas

¾ cup turkey breast, diced

¼ cup cranberry sauce

½ cup jack cheese, shredded

1 tsp. sage, chopped

2 tbsp. gravy, heated

½ cup mayonnaise

Directions

1. Place one tortilla on the Grill Pan. Top with turkey, cranberry sauce, jack cheese, and sage. Top with the second tortilla.

2. Grill on each side until cooked.

3. In a bowl, combine gravy and mayonnaise.

4. Serve warm tortillas with gravy.

Eric's Tip: Get some Texas toast and turn these quesadillas into a grilled cheese!

Greek Quesadilla

Ingredients

1 chicken breast, sliced in half

Greek Marinade

juice of ½ lemon

1 sprig oregano

½ tsp. salt

½ tsp. ground black pepper

2 tbsp. olive oil

---

2 (8-in.) tortillas

¼ cup feta cheese

½ cup jack cheese, shredded

2 pepperoncini peppers, sliced

½ cup cherry tomatoes, halved

2 tbsp. olives, halved

sour cream, to serve

Directions

1. In a dish, combine chicken with marinade ingredients. Marinate in the refrigerator for 20 minutes.

2. Grill chicken on both sides until done, about 3-4 minutes per side. Let cool before dicing into small pieces.

3. Arrange one tortilla onto the Grill Pan. Top with feta and jack cheeses, pepperoncini, cherry tomatoes, olives, and diced chicken. Finish with second tortilla.

4. Grill quesadilla on each side until golden.

5. Cut quesadilla and serve with sour cream.

Eric's Tip: Here is a dipping sauce that will make this even more flavorful. In a blender or food processor, combine 1 clove of garlic and ½ cup of plain yogurt with ½ cup of chopped cucumber, a ½ teaspoon of oregano, and the juice of half a lemon. Season to taste with salt and pepper.

Cheeseburger Quesadilla

Ingredients

1 lb. ground beef

1 tbsp. Worcestershire sauce

1 tbsp. garlic powder

1 onion, peeled & diced

6 (8-in.) flour tortillas

18 slices American cheese

3 pickles, sliced

¼ cup ketchup

¼ cup mustard

Directions

1. In a frying pan, sauté ground beef with Worcestershire sauce, garlic powder, and onions for about 10 minutes.

2. Place one tortilla on the Grill Pan. Layer with 3 slices American cheese, 1 pickle, ketchup, and mustard. Top with 3 more slices of cheese and a second tortilla.

3. Grill the quesadilla on both sides until golden. Repeat to make two more quesadillas.

4. Serve warm with your favorite side dish & Eric's dipping sauce (see tip).

Eric's Tip: My Not So Secret Dipping Sauce: combine 1 cup mayo, 3 tbsp. ketchup, 3 tbsp. relish, ¼ tsp. cayenne, 1 tsp. Dijon mustard, and ¼ tsp. garlic powder.

Vegetable Quesadilla

Ingredients

2 tbsp. margarine

2 (8-in.) flour tortillas

3 slices zucchini, grilled

3 mini peppers, grilled

4 Brussels sprouts, grilled

1 plum tomato, diced

¼ red onion, grilled

¼ jalapeño, diced

1 tbsp. cilantro, chopped

¾ cup shredded cheddar jack mix

2 tbsp. sour cream

½ tsp. lime zest

¼ tsp. sea salt

Directions

1. Butter both tortillas on one side only. Set aside.

2. Arrange one tortilla onto the Griddle Pan.

3. Top with vegetables and cheese.

4. Place second tortilla on top.

5. On medium heat, cook on both sides, about 4-5 minutes or until golden.

6. In a small dish, combine sour cream, lime zest, and salt.

7. Cut the quesadilla and top with sour cream before serving.

Griddle Recipe

Pizza

Wild Mushroom Asiago Pizza

BBQ Chicken Pizza

Pesto White Pizza

Chicken Ranch Pizza

Mexican Pizza

Sun-Dried Tomato Focaccia

Pulled Pork Pizza

Caramelized Onion, Pear
& Bleu Cheese Pizza

Spinach, Feta & Red Onion Pizza

Rosemary Garlic Focaccia

BLT Pizza

Margherita Pizza

Fig & Arugula Pizza

Wild Mushroom Asiago Pizza

SERVES 6

Ingredients

3 portobello mushrooms

10 shiitake mushrooms

10 oyster mushrooms

1 pizza dough, thin crust

16 slices Asiago cheese

3 tbsp. grana padano cheese, grated

4 cloves garlic, peeled & sliced

1 tsp. truffle salt

2 tbsp. extra virgin olive oil

Directions

1. Grill the mushrooms until tender. Chop and set aside.

2. Preheat the oven to 400° F.

3. Arrange dough to fit onto the Grill Pan. Grill both sides, then flip again.

4. Distribute both cheeses, chopped mushrooms, and garlic over the pizza. Sprinkle with truffle salt. Drizzle with olive oil.

5. Finish cooking in the oven for about 10 minutes.

6. Slice pizza before serving with your favorite side dishes.

Eric's Tip: I absolutely love dried porcini mushrooms! Soaking 1 oz. of dried porcinis in ½ cup warm water will add that umami flavor to the pizza.

BBQ Chicken Pizza

Ingredients

2 chicken breasts

½ cup BBQ sauce

1 red onion, peeled & sliced

2 tbsp. olive oil

1 pizza dough, thin crust

1 cup shredded cheddar

4 scallions, chopped

Directions

1. In a bowl, combine ¼ cup BBQ sauce with chicken. Grill until fully cooked. Allow to cool, then chop into pieces.

2. Preheat the oven to 400° F.

3. Toss the onions with olive oil. Grill to desired doneness.

4. Arrange dough to fit onto the Grill Pan. Grill one side of the pizza, then flip. Brush cooked side with remaining BBQ sauce. Top with cheddar cheese, red onion, and diced chicken.

5. Finish cooking in the oven for about 10 minutes.

6. Slice and sprinkle with scallions before serving.

Eric's Tip: Using a pre-made rotisserie chicken can save you some time if you don't want to cook the chicken breast.

Pesto White Pizza

Ingredients

1 pizza dough, thin crust

$^1/_3$ cup pesto sauce

1 cup ricotta

8 oz. fresh mozzarella, sliced thin

1 large Roma tomato, sliced thin
& cut into half-moons

2 tbsp. Parmesan cheese, grated

1 pinch red pepper flakes

salt and pepper, to taste

Directions

1. Preheat the oven to 450° F.

2. Arrange dough to fit onto the Grill Pan. Grill on medium heat until cooked on both sides.

3. Remove dough from heat. Brush pesto over the dough.
    Layer with ricotta, mozzarella, tomatoes, Parmesan, and red pepper flakes. Season with salt and pepper.

4. Cook in the oven until pizza is lightly golden and cheese is melted.

Eric's Tip: I love taking that leftover rotisserie chicken and adding it to this pizza.

Chicken Ranch Pizza

SERVES 6

Ingredients

1 pizza dough

2 cups cheddar, shredded

2 cups cooked rotisserie chicken, shredded

4 strips bacon, cooked crispy & crumbled

¼ cup scallions

½ cup ranch dressing

Directions

1. Arrange pizza dough to fit onto the Grill Pan.

2. Preheat the oven to 400° F.

3. On medium heat, grill pizza on both sides until golden.

4. Sprinkle shredded cheddar onto the dough. Top with chicken, bacon, and scallions.

5. Place the Grill Pan into the oven. Bake until the cheese is melted and the dough is cooked through.

6. Drizzle ranch dressing over the pizza immediately before serving.

Eric's Tip: Make it a club by topping with chopped lettuce, tomato and avocado!

Mexican Pizza

Ingredients

1 (8-in.) flour tortilla

½ cup salsa

1 cup shredded cheese,
Mexican blend

¼ cup black beans, drained
& rinsed

1 link fully cooked chorizo, cut into
thick medallions & quartered

To Serve

¼ cup scallions, chopped

2 tbsp. cilantro leaves

sliced jalapeño

2 tbsp. Mexican crema

Directions

1. Preheat the oven to 400° F.

2. Grill the tortilla for 2 or 3 minutes on each side.

3. Spread salsa around the tortilla. Top with cheese, then beans,
    and finally chorizo.

4. Bake in the oven until cheese has melted. Top with scallions, cilantro,
    and sliced jalapeño. Drizzle with crema immediately before serving.

Eric's Tip: For a lighter version you can substitute chorizo with turkey
or chicken sausage.

Sun-Dried Tomato Focaccia

SERVES 6

Ingredients

3 tbsp. extra virgin olive oil

4 cloves garlic, sliced

1 pizza dough

1 cup sun-dried tomatoes, hydrated

¼ cup Romano cheese, grated

1 tbsp. dried rosemary

1 tsp. dried oregano

1 tbsp. sea salt

Directions

1. In a sauté pan, cook garlic in olive oil until golden. Reserve remaining olive oil for later.

2. Arrange pizza dough to fit onto the Grill Pan. Grill on one side before flipping over.

3. Brush with olive oil from step 1.

4. Scatter sun-dried tomatoes evenly over the dough. Sprinkle with Romano cheese, rosemary, oregano, garlic, and sea salt.

5. Grill focaccia to desired crispness. Serve warm with your favorite dish or as a snack.

Eric's Tip: Allow your dough to sit out covered for about 15 minutes prior to rolling. It will be easier to work with when it's not cold, plus you will get a better rise.

Pulled Pork Pizza

Ingredients

2 cups pulled pork

⅓ cup BBQ sauce

1 pizza dough

1 cup cheddar, shredded

1 red onion, peeled & sliced thin

Chipotle Sauce

1 cup mayonnaise

2 chipotle peppers

Directions

1. Preheat the oven to 400° F.

2. Mix pulled pork together with BBQ sauce.

3. Arrange pizza dough to fit onto the Grill Pan. Grill on one side before flipping over.

4. Sprinkle pizza with pulled pork and then cheddar.

5. Cook in the oven for about 10 minutes.

6. Combine chipotles and mayonnaise in a blender. Blend until smooth.

7. Spread red onions over the pizza. Drizzle with chipotle sauce before cutting and serving.

Eric's Tip: Don't be afraid to add a little texture after cooking. I'll top this pizza with pre-made crispy fried onions.

Caramelized Onion, Pear & Bleu Cheese Pizza

SERVES 4-6

Ingredients

2 red onions, peeled & sliced

3 tbsp. butter

1 pizza dough, thin crust

2 pears, cored & sliced

1 cup bleu cheese

2 cups arugula

2 tbsp. extra virgin olive oil

½ tsp. sea salt

½ tsp. ground black pepper

Directions

1. In a sauté pan, caramelize red onions in butter.

2. Preheat the oven to 400° F.

3. On medium heat, grill the pizza dough on both sides to desired doneness.

4. Top pizza with pears and bleu cheese. Bake in the oven for 10 minutes.

5. Toss arugula with olive oil, sea salt, and pepper.

6. Top pizza with arugula immediately before serving.

Eric's Tip: Don't let the bleu cheese scare you away, it's amazing in this dish. There are many varieties, so talk to your local cheesemonger to find one that suits your taste.

Spinach, Feta & Red Onion Pizza

SERVES 6

Ingredients

1 thin crust pizza dough

5 oz. baby spinach

¼ cup extra virgin olive oil

1 clove garlic, peeled & minced

½ cup feta cheese, crumbled

1 small red onion, halved & sliced

¼ cup kalamata olives, halved

¼ cup sun-dried tomatoes, chopped

salt & pepper

Directions

1. Arrange pizza dough to fit onto the Grill Pan.

2. Preheat the oven to 400° F.

3. In a pan, sauté spinach lightly with olive oil and garlic.

4. On medium heat, grill the pizza on both sides until golden.

5. Sprinkle feta onto the dough. Top with spinach, red onion, olives, and sun-dried tomatoes. Add salt and pepper, to taste.

6. Place the Grill Pan into the oven. Bake until the cheese is melted and the dough is cooked through.

Eric's Tip: I love adding baby arugula to this pizza. Layer it under the feta before cooking, or use it as a garnish after cooking.

Rosemary Garlic Focaccia

SERVES 6

Ingredients

1 lb. pizza dough

¼ cup extra virgin olive oil

½ tbsp. sea salt, course

2 large sprigs rosemary, leaves removed

4 cloves garlic, peeled & thinly sliced

Directions

1. Arrange pizza dough to fit onto the Grill Pan.

2. Proof at room temperature for 45 minutes.

3. Preheat the oven to 450° F.

4. Use your fingers to make indentations in the dough.

5. Rub olive oil onto the dough. Top with sea salt, rosemary, and garlic. Bake for 10-12 minutes or until golden brown.

6. Serve with fresh salad as a side or topping.

Eric's Tip: This focaccia can be repurposed into sandwich bread, croutons or pizza!

BLT Pizza

Ingredients

1 pizza crust, thin

9 slices provolone cheese

½ lb. bacon, grilled
(reserve 2 tbsp. grease)

12 tomato slices

1 red onion, peeled, sliced,
& grilled

2 cups lettuce, shredded

2 tbsp. mayonnaise

Directions

1. Preheat the oven to 400° F.

2. Arrange pizza dough to fit onto the Grill Pan. Grill both sides
to desired doneness.

3. Top with the cheese and bacon grease. Bake in the oven for 10 minutes.

4. Layer pizza with bacon, tomato, onion, and lettuce. Drizzle with
mayonnaise before serving.

Eric's Tip: Don't forget the diced ripe avocado! And feel free to make it
lighter by using grilled chicken or turkey bacon.

Margherita Pizza

Ingredients

1 pizza dough, thin crust

2 tbsp. basil pesto

2 tomatoes, vine ripe, sliced

14 slices fresh mozzarella

1 clove garlic, peeled & sliced thin

1 tbsp. olive oil

Directions

1. Preheat the Griddle Pan on high heat.

2. Roll the pizza dough to fit onto the Pan. Cook on one side until golden.

3. Flip the dough. Spread the pesto on top followed by tomato slices, mozzarella slices, and garlic. Drizzle with olive oil.

4. Preheat the broiler.

5. Place the Pan under broiler to melt the cheese and toast the garlic.

Griddle Recipe

Fig & Arugula Pizza

Ingredients

1 thin crust pizza dough

3 tbsp. fig spread

½ cup crumbled bleu cheese

1 cup arugula

2 tbsp. extra virgin olive oil

Directions

1. Preheat the Griddle Pan on high heat.

2. Roll the pizza dough to fit onto the Pan. Cook on one side until golden.

3. Flip the dough and spread with fig paste. Top with crumbled bleu cheese.

4. Cook until crispy and golden.

5. Remove from Pan. Top with arugula and drizzle with extra virgin olive oil before serving.

Griddle Recipe

Chicken

Sesame Ginger Sticky Wings

SERVES 4

Ingredients

2 lb. chicken wings, split

Sesame Ginger Marinade

1 cup sweet chili sauce

1 tbsp. ginger

1 tbsp. sesame oil

½ tbsp. chili paste

2 tbsp. honey

1 tbsp. lime juice

Garnish

1 tbsp. sesame seeds

scallions, chopped

Directions

1. Preheat the oven to 375° F.

2. On medium heat, grill the wings on both sides.

3. Marinade: in a bowl, combine sweet chili sauce, ginger, sesame oil, chili paste, honey, and lime juice.

4. Grill wings until fully cooked and crispy. Toss in sesame ginger marinade.

5. Sprinkle with sesame seeds and scallions before serving.

Eric's Tip: This marinade works well with chicken breasts and thighs if you want to add it to a salad, sandwich or tacos.

Grill Press
Accessory is required for this recipe.

SERVES 2

Ingredients

Chili Lime Spice

2 tbsp. chili powder

1 tsp. coriander

1 tsp. cumin

1 tsp. paprika

2 tsp. garlic powder

1 tsp. onion powder

3 tbsp. lime juice

2 tsp. lime zest

¼ cup olive oil

½ tbsp. sea salt

1 tsp. ground black pepper

3 lb. whole chicken,
backbone removed

Chili Lime Spatchcock Chicken

Directions

1. Chili lime spice: in a bowl, combine all spice ingredients.

2. Arrange the chicken upside-down in a shallow pan. Season with spice mix.

3. Grill chicken on medium heat. Place the **Grill Press** on top of the chicken.

4. Baste with spice mix. Preheat the oven to 375° F.

5. Flip the chicken over. Bake in the oven until internal temperature reaches 165° F.

6. Allow chicken to rest for 15 minutes before serving.

Eric's Tip: You always want to let cooked meat rest before slicing so the juices redistribute back into the meat. If you cut it too soon, all the juice will run out which will result in a dry chicken.

Tomato & Pesto Stuffed Chicken Breast

Ingredients

Pesto

1 cup basil

3 tbsp. cup parsley

2 tbsp. pine nuts, toasted

2 cloves garlic

¼ cup Parmesan cheese, grated

½ cup extra virgin olive oil

1 tsp. sea salt

¼ tsp. black pepper

Chicken

4 chicken breasts, boneless
& skinless

salt and pepper, to taste

1 tbsp. extra virgin olive oil

Stuffing

2 Roma tomatoes, sliced
into rounds

8 oz. fresh mozzarella, sliced
into rounds

1 cup baby spinach

Directions

1. Chop all pesto ingredients in a food processor.

2. Preheat the oven to 400° F.

3. Slice the chicken lengthwise to make a pocket for the stuffing.

4. Rub the inside of each breast with pesto. Layer with tomato, mozzarella cheese, and spinach.

5. Season the outside of the chicken with salt and pepper, to taste. Brush with olive oil.

6. Place the Grill Pan on high heat.

7. Grill the chicken breasts for 4-5 minutes on each side. Bake in the oven until chicken reaches an internal temperature of 165° F.

8. Allow chicken to rest for 5 minutes before slicing and serving.

Eric's Tip: Serve this chicken in between some fresh baked focaccia for the best Italian grinder.

Tomato & Olive Grilled Thighs

SERVES 4

Ingredients

Marinade

½ onion, peeled & minced

2 cloves garlic, peeled & minced

2 sprigs rosemary

3 sprigs thyme

¼ cup apple cider vinegar

½ cup olive oil

2 tbsp. soy sauce

3 tbsp. honey

1 tsp. ground black pepper

———————

8 chicken thighs

Tomato and Olive Salad

3 tomatoes, diced

½ cup kalamata olives, chopped

1 clove garlic, peeled & minced

¼ red onion, peeled & minced

½ head fennel, diced small

6 basil leaves, chopped

1 tsp. sea salt

½ tsp. ground black pepper

Directions

1. Combine all marinade ingredients in a bowl. Marinate chicken in the refrigerator for 6 hours.

2. Preheat the oven to 350° F.

3. Grill chicken on both sides for about 7 minutes each.

4. Place the Grill Pan into the oven. Cook chicken until internal temperature reaches 165° F.

5. Combine tomato and olive salad ingredients in a bowl. Plate with chicken before serving.

Eric's Tip: I love to pair this dish with grilled romaine hearts or radicchio.

Grill Press
Accessory is required for this recipe.

SERVES 2

Ingredients

Spicy BBQ Sauce

1 cup BBQ sauce

2 tbsp. sriracha sauce

½ tsp. liquid smoke

1 tsp. garlic powder

1 tsp. onion powder

1 tsp. salt

1 tsp. ground black pepper

3 lb. whole chicken,
backbone removed

Spicy BBQ Brick Chicken

Directions

1. In a bowl, mix together all sauce ingredients. Pour over the chicken.

2. Preheat the oven to 350° F.

3. Arrange the chicken bone-side down onto the Grill Pan. Top with the **Grill Press**. Cook for about 7 minutes on each side.

4. Cook in the oven (do not remove **Grill Press**) about 20 minutes or until internal temperature reaches 165° F.

Eric's Tip: When I make brick chicken, I'll make sure to rub some of the marinade between the meat and skin.

Tandoori Chicken Skewers

SERVES 8

Ingredients

Tandoori Marinade

1 cup yogurt

1 ½ tsp. garam masala

¼ tsp. cayenne pepper

2 tbsp. yellow onion, grated

1 tsp. garlic, grated

1 tsp. ginger, grated

juice of ½ lemon

2 lb. chicken breast, trimmed & cubed

scallions, for garnish

Directions

1. Tandoori marinade: in a bowl, combine yogurt, garam masala, cayenne, onion, garlic, ginger, and lemon juice.

2. Marinate chicken overnight in the refrigerator.

3. Set the Grill Pan on medium heat. Skewer the chicken.

4. Grill chicken on all sides until cooked to 165° F internal temperature.

5. Garnish with scallions. Serve with a salad or traditional side dishes.

Eric's Tip: For the best chicken salad, chill in the refrigerator after grilling. Hand shred the chicken, then mix with chopped onion, celery, dried cranberries, and a touch of mayonnaise.

Sweet & Spicy Smoked Chicken Thighs

SERVES 4

Ingredients

2 lb. chicken thighs

Sweet & Spicy Sauce

⅓ cup molasses

1 tbsp. cider vinegar

2 tbsp. butter, melted

2 cloves garlic, peeled & minced

½ onion, peeled & minced

1 tsp. red pepper flakes

1 tsp. hot pepper sauce

½ tsp. liquid smoke

Directions

1. Preheat the oven to 375° F.

2. Grill chicken thighs on medium heat on both sides.

3. Combine sauce ingredients in a bowl.

4. Coat chicken thighs with sauce and return to the Grill Pan.

5. Bake until chicken reaches 165° F internal temperature. Remove from the oven and dip back into the sauce. Return to the oven for an additional five minutes.

6. Serve chicken thighs with your favorite vegetable.

Eric's Tip: If you want to give these thighs an autumnal feel, replace molasses with 5 cups fresh apple cider cooked down to ⅓ cup.

Pesto Chicken Paillard

Ingredients

2 chicken breasts, sliced lengthwise & pounded ¼ in. thick

4 tbsp. pesto

Marinade

¼ cup olive oil

2 tbsp. red wine vinegar

½ tsp. ground black pepper

1 tsp. sea salt

4 tbsp. pesto

Arugula Salad

1 cup arugula

2 cups mesclun mix

3 tbsp. extra virgin olive oil

½ lemon, juiced

½ tsp. ground black pepper

½ tsp. sea salt

¼ cup Parmigiano-Reggiano cheese, shaved

½ cup cherry tomatoes, halved

Directions

1. Combine chicken with marinade ingredients for 1-2 hours.

2. Grill chicken until done. Chicken will cook quickly as it is very thin.

3. Remove chicken from the Grill Pan. Brush with pesto.

4. Combine salad ingredients in a large bowl. Toss.

5. Serve chicken over greens.

Eric's Tip: I love tossing the salad with fresh cooked pasta to gently wilt the greens to make it an entrée.

Asian BBQ Thighs

SERVES 4

Ingredients

Asian BBQ Sauce

$^2/_3$ cup hoisin sauce

¼ cup molasses

$^1/_3$ cup honey

¼ cup rice vinegar

1 tsp. five-spice powder

2 cloves garlic, minced

1 tsp. ginger, minced

1 shallot, minced

1 tsp. fish sauce

---

8 chicken thighs, skinless
& boneless

Directions

1. Combine all BBQ sauce ingredients with chicken in a bowl. Marinate in the refrigerator for 6 hours.

2. Heat the Grill Pan on medium. Preheat the oven to 375° F.

3. Grill the chicken on both sides while basting with BBQ sauce.

4. Bake in the oven until chicken reaches 165° F internal temperature.

5. Serve with salad or vegetables.

Eric's Tip: The kids love when I pick up a pack of mini buns and coleslaw to turn these into Asian chicken sliders.

Italian Chicken & Panzanella

SERVES 2-4

Ingredients

Marinade

1 tbsp. Italian seasoning

1 tsp. sea salt

1 tsp. black pepper

1 tsp. garlic powder

1 tsp. onion powder

2 tbsp. olive oil

2 chicken breasts, trimmed

Panzanella Salad

½ baguette, sliced lengthwise

1 pint grape tomatoes

1 seedless cucumber, cubed

2 tbsp. parsley, chopped

4 large basil leaves, chiffonade

¼ cup red wine vinegar

½ cup extra virgin olive oil

1 tsp. salt

1 tsp. ground black pepper

1 clove garlic, peeled & minced

1 red onion, peeled & sliced thin

Directions

1. In a bowl, combine marinade ingredients. Rub the chicken on both sides.

2. Grill chicken for 5-7 minutes on each side or until done.

3. Grill the baguette until crispy. Cut into cubes.

4. Slice the chicken. Toss with remaining salad ingredients and bread before serving.

Eric's Tip: Panzanella salad was originally created by the resourceful Italian Grandmothers to use up day-old bread.

Blackened Chicken Breast with Mango Salsa

SERVES 6

Ingredients

6 chicken breasts, boneless

3-4 tbsp. blackened seasoning

Mango Salsa

1 mango, peeled & diced small

¼ red onion, diced

¼ red pepper, diced

1 tbsp. cilantro, chopped

¼ jalapeño, minced

2 tbsp. mango juice

—————

2 tbsp. olive oil

Directions

1. Season the chicken generously with blackened spice.

2. Combine mango salsa ingredients in a bowl. Set aside.

3. Preheat the Griddle Pan on high heat for 5 minutes.

4. Add olive oil to coat Pan. Blacken chicken on both sides until cooked.

5. Slice chicken and serve with mango salsa.

Griddle Recipe

Whole Chicken with Eric's Poultry Rub

SERVES 4

Ingredients

Eric's Poultry Rub

2 tbsp. crushed sea salt

2 tbsp. paprika

1 tsp. sugar

1 tbsp. turmeric

2 tsp. garlic powder

2 tsp. granulated dried onion

1 tbsp. ground thyme

1 tsp. mustard powder

½ tsp. cayenne

2 tsp. dried lemon peel

1 tbsp. black ground pepper

---

3 lb. chicken, whole

3 tbsp. olive oil

1 lemon, quartered

1 orange, quartered

Directions

1. Preheat the oven to 350° F.

2. In a bowl, mix rub ingredients.

3. Distribute rub over the entire chicken, then coat with olive oil.

4. Fill chicken cavity with lemon and orange quarters. Arrange chicken onto the Grill Pan.

5. Cook in the oven until internal temperature reaches 165° F.

6. Let chicken rest for 15 minutes before slicing and serving.

7. Serve with your favorite vegetable or grilled onions and Brussels Sprouts.

Eric's Tip: Please don't think this is only good on chicken. I've used it on everything from salmon to pork chops. You can also mix it into your mayo for a good kick on your sandwich!

Grilled Salmon
with Cider & Shallots

Shrimp Tacos
& Cilantro Aioli

Grilled Salmon
& Chorizo Vinaigrette

Shrimp & Sausage Skewers

Sweet & Spicy
Bacon-Wrapped Catfish

Mustard-Marinated Swordfish
with Spinach

Flounder Spaghetti

Tilapia & Corn Salsa

Grilled Tuna & Lime
Cilantro Butter Sauce

Curry Coconut Scallops

Grilled Mahi Mahi
with Eric's Fish Rub

Sweet Sriracha Shrimp Tacos

Garlic Lime Shrimp

Salmon with Mustard-Dill
Compound Butter

Fish & Seafood

Grilled Salmon with Cider & Shallots

SERVES 6

Ingredients

6 (5-oz.) salmon fillets

Marinade

1 shallot peeled & chopped

1 tbsp. soy sauce

2 tbsp. apple cider

1 tsp. peppercorns, crushed

2 sprigs tarragon, chopped

juice of 1 lemon

Cider & Shallot Sauce

2 tbsp. butter

4 shallot, peeled & sliced

1 cup cider

¼ cup white wine

1 sprig tarragon, chopped

1 tbsp. parsley, chopped

1 bay leaf

½ tsp sea salt

¼ tsp. ground black pepper

Directions

1. In a bowl, combine salmon with marinade ingredients. Marinate in the refrigerator for one hour.

2. Remove salmon from marinade. Pat dry with a paper towel. Grill for about 6 minutes per side or until desired doneness.

3. Make the sauce: in a frying pan, sauté shallots in butter until translucent.

4. Add remaining sauce ingredients. Reduce by two-thirds.

5. Spoon sauce over the salmon. Serve with your favorite side dish.

Eric's Tip: Making sure the fish is completely dry from the marinade is key to beautiful grill marks. For that professional restaurant looking cross-hatch, turn the salmon a quarter turn after the initial 3 minutes of grilling on the first side.

Shrimp Tacos & Cilantro Aioli

SERVES 4

Ingredients

1 lb. shrimp, 21-25 size, peeled & deveined

1 tbsp. seafood seasoning

1 tsp. onion powder

½ tsp. sea salt

½ tsp. ground black pepper

2 tbsp. extra virgin olive oil

Cilantro Aioli

¼ cup mayonnaise

1 tsp. hot sauce

1 tbsp. cilantro, chopped

1 clove fresh garlic chopped

4 (6-in.) flour tortillas

fresh cilantro & lime, for serving

Taco Toppings

1 cup cabbage, chopped

1 yellow pepper, seeded & diced

¼ red onion, peeled & minced

1 plum tomato, diced & chopped

Directions

1. Toss the shrimp with seafood seasoning, onion powder, sea salt, pepper, and olive oil. Grill on both sides to desired doneness.

2. In a bowl, mix together aioli ingredients. Set aside.

3. Assemble the tacos: spread some aioli onto each tortilla. Layer with cabbage, yellow pepper, onion, tomato, and shrimp.

4. Serve with limes and fresh cilantro leaves.

Eric's Tip: Depending on my mood and what's fresh at the market, I'll substitute the shrimp for scallops or lobster. Don't forget the crumbled queso fresco!

Grilled Salmon & Chorizo Vinaigrette

SERVES 4

Ingredients

Chorizo Vinaigrette

½ cup extra virgin olive oil

2 links chorizo, diced

2 tsp. garlic, minced

1 pinch ground coriander

¼ cup scallions

1 tbsp. cilantro, chopped

juice of 1 lime

salt and pepper

—

4 (6-oz.) salmon fillets, skin on

salt and pepper

Directions

1. In a frying pan, crisp the chorizo in olive oil. Remove from heat.

2. Add garlic and coriander to the pan. Stir. Cool to room temperature. Stir in scallions, cilantro, and lime juice. Season with salt and pepper, to taste.

3. Place the Grill Pan on medium heat. Season salmon with salt and pepper.

4. Grill salmon, skin side down, for 4-5 minutes per side until done.

5. Serve fillets with chorizo vinaigrette.

Eric's Tip: Serve this over a delicious mushroom risotto or mixed greens salad. It works both hot and cold!

Shrimp & Sausage Skewers

SERVES 4

Ingredients

24 shrimp, 16-20 size, peeled & deveined

1 lime, juiced

1 clove garlic, peeled & minced

½ tsp. sea salt

½ tsp. ground black pepper

6 sprigs cilantro, chopped

2 chorizo sausage links, sliced

Directions

1. Combine shrimp with lime juice, garlic, sea salt, pepper, and cilantro. Marinate in the refrigerator for 1 hour.

2. Assemble skewers with alternating pieces of shrimp and sausage.

3. Grill skewers on each side, about 4-5 minutes per side.

4. Serve skewers with rice or your favorite side dish.

Eric's Tip: Using smoked or cured sausage will prevent the shrimp from over cooking. If you can only get raw sausage, pre-cook and cool then slice into chunks.

Sweet & Spicy Bacon-Wrapped Catfish

SERVES 2

Ingredients

2 cups spinach

2 pc. catfish

4 slices bacon

Sweet & Spicy Glaze

2 tbsp. sweet chili sauce

1 tbsp. sweet soy sauce

1 tbsp. rice vinegar

1 tsp. chipotle powder

½ onion, peeled & minced

Directions

1. Steam spinach. Let cool.

2. Lay each catfish fillet flat. Spoon half of the spinach on top of each. Roll fillet around spinach to make a roulade.

3. Preheat the oven to 400° F.

4. Wrap two slices bacon around each roulade. Grill on medium heat, about 5 minutes per side.

5. Combine glaze ingredients in a bowl. Spoon generously over fish.

6. Place the Grill Pan into the oven for 8-10 minutes or until fish is cooked.

7. Serve with any remaining glaze and your favorite side dish.

Eric's Tip: Call me crazy, but when I was developing this recipe, I put the catfish in a nice fresh long roll to make an awesome Po' Boy. Just add some shredded lettuce and sliced tomato!

Mustard-Marinated Swordfish with Spinach

SERVES 8

Ingredients

Mustard Marinade

2 shallots, peeled & minced

1 tbsp. mustard seeds

¼ cup white wine vinegar

2 sprigs tarragon

¾ cup olive oil

½ tbsp. honey

1 tsp. sea salt

½ tsp. black peppercorns, crushed

---

8 (6-oz.) swordfish steaks

10 cups spinach, steamed

½ cup cherry tomatoes, cut in half, for garnish

Directions

1. Mustard marinade: boil the shallot, mustard seeds, vinegar, and tarragon in a saucepan for 2-3 minutes. Set aside to cool.

2. Add the olive oil, honey, sea salt, and peppercorns. Mix well.

3. Pour half of the marinade over the swordfish steaks. Reserve remaining marinade for serving.

4. Allow fish to marinate in the refrigerator for 3 hours.

5. Heat the Grill Pan on high heat. Grill swordfish steaks on each side until done, about 3-4 minutes. Cooking time may vary depending on thickness.

6. Plate swordfish over spinach with remaining marinade. Sprinkle with cherry tomatoes before serving.

Eric's Tip: You can use any quality IQF (individually quick frozen) fish in this recipe such as mahi mahi, tuna, or salmon. Thaw and adjust grilling time according to directions.

Flounder Spaghetti

SERVES 6

Ingredients

1 lb. spaghetti

1 lb. flounder fillet

4 cloves garlic, sliced

¼ cup extra virgin olive oil

½ cup parsley, chopped

½ tsp. red pepper flakes

salt and pepper

lemon wedges, for serving

Directions

1. Cook spaghetti according to the box directions.

2. Grill flounder on medium heat to desired doneness.

3. In a separate pot, sauté the garlic in olive oil until lightly golden.

4. Add cooked pasta, parsley, red pepper flakes, and flounder to the pot. Season with salt and pepper.

5. Serve spaghetti with lemon wedges.

Eric's Tip: Every time I make this, I have a craving to add broccoli rabe into the pasta. Spinach and kale will also work well and add that South Philly flair!

Tilapia & Corn Salsa

Ingredients

Corn Salsa

3 ears corn, grilled

4 scallions, chopped

6 sprigs cilantro, chopped

1 lime, juiced

1 tsp sea salt

½ red pepper, seeded & chopped

½ jalapeño, chopped

4 tilapia fillets

Eric's Fish Rub

½ tsp. sea salt

½ tsp. onion powder

½ tsp. thyme

½ tsp. tarragon

½ tbsp. dried parsley

½ tbsp. dried cilantro

½ tsp. ground white pepper

1 tsp. dried lemon peel

½ tsp. celery seed

Directions

1. Remove corn from the cob. Combine with salsa ingredients in a bowl. Toss and set aside.

2. Rub tilapia gently with fish rub. Grill 2-4 minutes per side.

3. Serve with corn salsa.

Eric's Tip: I love experimenting with the fish rub. I'll add some cayenne or dried habanero for an extra kick. For a Mediterranean feel, I'll throw in some ground fennel and anise seed.

Grilled Tuna & Lime Cilantro Butter Sauce

SERVES 4

Ingredients

4 (6-oz.) tuna steaks, center cut

Marinade

1 tbsp. coriander, seeds

1 tbsp. ground black pepper

1 tbsp. garlic powder

3 tbsp. grape seed oil

2 tbsp. soy sauce

1 lime, juiced

Cilantro Lime Butter Sauce

1 stick butter

1 shallot, peeled & chopped

1 lime, juiced

½ tsp coriander powder

½ tsp. sriracha sauce

½ tsp. sea salt

½ tsp. chipotle powder

3 tbsp. cilantro, chopped

Directions

1. In a bowl, combine tuna with marinade ingredients. Marinate in the refrigerator for 30 minutes.

2. Remove tuna from marinade. Pat dry with paper towels.

3. Grill tuna steaks on both sides, about 3 minutes each.

4. In a saucepan, sauté shallot with 2 tbsp. butter. Add lime juice, coriander, sriracha, sea salt, and chipotle powder. Cook until reduced by half, then turn off the heat. Whisk in remaining butter with the chopped cilantro.

5. Spoon sauce generously over sliced tuna before serving.

Eric's Tip: In most recipes, substitutions can be made. In this, I really stand firm in using a high-quality tuna steak. Cooking the tuna to a nice medium rare is my favorite preference. Most markets now carry sushi-grade tuna so don't skimp and treat yourself!

Curry Coconut Scallops

SERVES 4

Ingredients

Coconut Curry Sauce

1 tbsp. olive oil

2 cloves garlic, peeled & minced

2 tbsp. red curry

1 can coconut milk

2 scallions, chopped

½ lime, juiced

1 tbsp. fish sauce

---

2 ½ lb. scallops

1 tbsp. cumin

1 tbsp. sea salt

1 tbsp. ground black pepper

scallions, chopped, for garnish

Directions

1. Sauce: in a saucepan, sauté the garlic in olive oil for 2 minutes or until slightly golden.

2. Add remaining sauce ingredients. Cook until slightly thickened.

3. Season scallops with cumin, sea salt, and pepper. Grill to desired doneness.

4. Serve scallops with coconut curry sauce. Garnish with scallions.

Eric's Tip: I love to serve these scallops over Thai rice noodles garnished with fresh bean sprouts and cilantro.

Grilled Mahi Mahi with Eric's Fish Rub

SERVES 4

Ingredients

Eric's Fish Rub

1 tbsp. crushed sea salt

1 tbsp. onion powder

1 tsp. thyme

2 tsp. tarragon

1 tbsp. dried parsley

1 tbsp. dried chives

1 tbsp. ground white pepper

1 tbsp. dried lemon peel

1 tsp. celery seed

4 fillets mahi mahi

Directions

1. In a bowl, combine the spices. Rub evenly over both sides of the mahi mahi.

2. Grill to desired doneness.

3. Serve mahi mahi with Grilled Peach & Pineapple Salsa.

Eric's Tip: Serve with warm flour tortillas and cabbage slaw for fantastic tacos.

Sweet Sriracha Shrimp Tacos

SERVES 4

Ingredients

1 lb. shrimp, 21-25 size, peeled & deveined

1 tsp. sriracha powder

1 tsp. onion powder

½ tsp. coriander, ground

4 (6-in.) flour tortillas

Sriracha Sauce

1 tsp. sriracha sauce

¼ cup mayonnaise

1 tsp. honey

1 tsp. lime juice

1 tbsp. cilantro, chopped

Toppings

1 cup red cabbage, chopped

1 avocado, sliced & pitted

½ cup mango, diced

4 scallions, chopped

¼ red onion, peeled & chopped

lime wedges, to serve

cilantro leaves, to serve

Directions

1. Toss the shrimp with sriracha powder, onion powder, and coriander. Grill to desired doneness.

2. In a bowl, combine sauce ingredients and set aside.

3. Assemble the tacos: spread sriracha onto each tortilla. Layer with cabbage, avocado, mango, scallion, red onion, and shrimp.

4. Serve tacos with limes and fresh cilantro leaves.

Eric's Tip: Substitute the shrimp for cubed salmon or swordfish for a different flavor profile.

Garlic Lime Shrimp

Ingredients

2 lb. shrimp, 16-20 size, peeled & deveined

2 limes, zested & juiced

¼ cup olive oil

2 tbsp. cilantro, chopped

2 cloves garlic, minced

¼ tsp. red pepper flakes

Directions

1. Combine all ingredients in a plastic bag. Refrigerate for 2 hours.

2. Preheat the Griddle Pan on medium heat for 5 minutes.

3. Remove shrimp from the marinade and pat dry with paper towels.

4. Cook shrimp on each side until done.

5. Serve shrimp with rice. Use leftovers for tacos.

Griddle Recipe

Salmon with Mustard-Dill Compound Butter

SERVES 6

Ingredients

6 salmon fillets

Marinade

¼ cup olive oil

2 tbsp. soy sauce

1 lemon, juiced

1 shallot, peeled & minced

Compound Butter

1 stick salted butter

1 tbsp. Dijon mustard

½ tsp. ground black pepper

1 shallot, peeled & minced

1 tbsp. chopped fresh dill

Directions

1. In a sealed plastic bag, combine fish with all of the marinade ingredients. Place in the refrigerator.

2. In a bowl, mix compound butter ingredients together. Set aside.

3. Preheat the Griddle Pan on medium heat.

4. Remove salmon from marinade. Pat dry with paper towels.

5. Cook the salmon on all sides until done.

6. Top each fillet with a tablespoon of compound butter before serving.

Griddle Recipe

24-Hour Marinated
Flat Iron Steaks

Herb-Grilled London Broil

Porcini-Crusted Rack of Lamb

Pork Chops
with Dried Plums & Shallots

Grilled Cowboy Steak
with Eric's Herb Salt Rub

Cherry Tomato Pork Tenderloin

Chimichurri Sirloin Steak

Mediterranean Pork Chops

5-Spice Dry Rub Ribs

Lamb Loin Chops
with Eric's Red Meat Rub

Eric's Surf & Turf

Grilled Skirt Steak
with Salsa Verde

Hanger Steak
& Green Peppercorn Butter

Flank Steak
with Balsamic Onion Dressing

Grilled Filet
with Porcini Compound Butter

Filet with Mushrooms
& Shallots

Meats

24-Hour Marinated Flat Iron Steaks

SERVES 4

Ingredients

2 lb. flat iron steak

Marinade

1 clove garlic, peeled & chopped

1 shallot, peeled & chopped

1 tsp. ground black pepper

1 tsp. sea salt

3 tbsp. balsamic vinegar

¼ cup extra virgin olive oil

2 sprigs rosemary

Eric's Herb Salt Rub

1 cup course ground sea salt

2 tbsp. black peppercorns

3 sprigs rosemary

4 sprigs thyme

1 sprig sage

2 sprigs tarragon

1 clove garlic, peeled

Directions

1. In a plastic lock bag, combine all marinade ingredients with steak. Refrigerate overnight.

2. Grill steak to desired temperature.

3. Let rest 10 minutes before slicing. Drizzle with extra virgin olive oil and sprinkle with Eric's Herb Salt before serving.

Eric's Tip: Flat Iron steaks cook quickly so be careful not to overcook. About 5-7 minutes per side should get you to a nice medium rare. I love this steak chilled the next day in a sandwich or salad.

Herb-Grilled London Broil

SERVES 4

Ingredients

2 sprigs rosemary

4 sprigs thyme

¼ cup pesto

2 tbsp. sea salt

1 tbsp. course ground black pepper

2 tbsp. extra virgin olive oil

3 lb. London broil

Directions

1. In a bowl, combine all spice ingredients with pesto and olive oil. Rub onto both sides of the steak. Refrigerate for 2 hours.

2. Grill London broil for about 7 minutes per side or to desired temperature.

3. Let rest for 10 minutes before slicing thin.

4. Serve with your favorite side dish or slice for a delicious sandwich.

Eric's Tip: If you want an extra special treat, make yourself a London broil club sandwich!

Porcini-Crusted Rack of Lamb

SERVES 2

Ingredients

Porcini Crust

¼ cup dried porcini mushrooms, blended to a powder

1 cup breadcrumbs

3 tbsp. Parmesan cheese

2 tbsp. parsley, chopped

1 tbsp. mint, chopped

---

1 rack of lamb, domestic

1 tbsp. olive oil

½ tsp. sea salt

½ tsp. ground black pepper

Directions

1. Porcini crust: combine porcini powder, breadcrumbs, Parmesan cheese, parsley, and mint in a bowl. Set aside.

2. Preheat the oven to 400° F.

3. Brush lamb with olive oil. Season with salt and pepper. Press porcini crust onto the lamb.

4. Arrange lamb carefully onto the Grill Pan. Cook in the oven to desired doneness.

5. Let rest before serving.

Eric's Tip: If you can't find a rack of lamb you can also use chops or even skewer lamb cubes.

Pork Chops with Dried Plums & Shallots

SERVES 6

Ingredients

1 cup dried plums

1 cup red wine

1 tbsp. butter

2 shallots, peeled & sliced

3 sprigs thyme

½ cup port wine

½ cup chicken broth

⅓ cup rice wine vinegar

¼ cup cream

6 center cut pork chops

1 tbsp. sea salt

½ tbsp. ground black pepper

Directions

1. In a small bowl, combine dried plums with red wine. Soak for 30 minutes.

2. In a saucepan, sauté shallots in butter for 2 minutes or until tender.

3. Add plums, thyme, port wine, chicken broth, and rice wine vinegar to shallots. Cook until reduced by half.

4. Add the cream. Reduce again until slightly thickened. Set aside.

5. Season pork chops with salt and pepper. Grill to desired doneness.

6. Drizzle pork chops with sauce and plums.

7. Serve with grilled carrots or your favorite vegetable.

Eric's Tip: With the availability of dried fruits, the variations are almost endless. If you don't like dried plums, use dried figs. If you don't like figs, use dried apricots.

Grilled Cowboy Steak with Eric's Herb Salt Rub

SERVES 2

Ingredients

Eric's Herb Salt Rub

1 cup course ground sea salt

2 tbsp. black peppercorns

3 sprigs rosemary

4 sprigs thyme

1 sprig sage

2 sprigs tarragon

1 clove garlic, peeled

---

2 lb. cowboy steak (bone-in, rib eye, trimmed)

Directions

1. Remove stems from all of the herbs. Blend salt rub ingredients together in a blender.

2. Preheat the oven to 400°F.

3. Rub the steak with ½ tbsp. salt rub on each side. Any remaining rub can be kept in a sealed container and used for meat or fish.

4. Grill steak on each side for 7 minutes.

5. Put the Grill Pan into the oven. Cook steak to desired temperature.

6. Let rest for 10 minutes before slicing and serving.

Eric's Tip: While the steak is resting on a separate plate, degrease the pan and then deglaze with 1 cup of white wine and reduce. Remove the pan from the heat and swirl in 2 tablespoons of butter for some awesome sauce!

Cherry Tomato Pork Tenderloin

SERVES 2

Ingredients

Marinade

1 clove garlic, peeled & minced

3 tbsp. olive oil

2 sprigs rosemary, chopped

1 tbsp. cider vinegar

1 tsp. sea salt

1 tsp. ground black pepper

---

2 lb. pork tenderloin

Sauce

1 tbsp. olive oil

1 clove garlic, peeled & minced

1 pint cherry tomatoes, halved

1 sprig tarragon, chopped

½ cup kalamata olives, halved

½ cup chicken broth

¼ cup white wine

1 tbsp. white balsamic vinegar

1 tbsp. honey

1 tsp. Dijon mustard

2 tbsp. butter

Directions

1. Combine marinade ingredients. Marinate pork in the refrigerator for 1 hour.

2. Grill until internal temperature reaches 165° F.

3. Sauce: in a saucepot, sauté the garlic in olive oil until lightly golden.

4. Add tomatoes and toss for 2 minutes. Add remaining sauce ingredients and reduce by half.

5. Spoon sauce over pork tenderloin before serving.

Eric's Tip: Allow pork tenderloin to rest for 15 min before slicing.

Chimichurri Sirloin Steak

Ingredients

Chimichurri Sauce

½ cup fresh Italian parsley

¼ cup olive oil

2 tbsp. red wine vinegar

¼ cup fresh cilantro

1 garlic clove, peeled

½ tsp. dried crushed red pepper

½ tsp. ground cumin

½ tsp. salt

---

2 (12-oz.) sirloin steaks
(NY strip steak)

1 tsp. sea salt

1 tsp. course ground black pepper

Directions

1. Combine all sauce ingredients together in a blender. Blend until well incorporated.

2. Season steaks with sea salt and pepper. Grill on medium heat, about 7 minutes on each side, or to desired doneness.

3. Let steaks rest for 10 minutes before slicing.

4. Plate sliced steak. Top with chimichurri sauce immediately before serving.

Eric's Tip: If you aren't a fan of cilantro, you can substitute any herb such as basil or thyme. You can make a Chimichurri Rojo by adding tomato or red pepper purée.

Mediterranean Pork Chops

SERVES 6

Ingredients

6 pork chops, thick cut

¼ cup olive oil

1 tbsp. sea salt

1 tsp. ground black pepper

Salad

½ cup kalamata olives

1 clove garlic, peeled & minced

1 pint cherry tomatoes, quartered

4 cups feta cheese

3 tbsp. red wine vinegar

1 sprig oregano, fresh

¼ cup extra virgin olive oil

1 cup cannellini beans

Directions

1. Rub pork chops with olive oil, sea salt, and pepper.

2. Grill about 5-7 minutes per side or until internal temperature reaches 165° F.

3. In a bowl, combine all salad ingredients. Toss.

4. Serve pork chops with salad and your favorite side dishes.

Eric's Tip: I love spooning the salad over couscous or tabbouleh for a complete meal.

5-Spice Dry Rub Ribs

Ingredients

Dry Rub

¼ cup five-spice

¼ cup brown sugar

2 tbsp. onion powder

2 tbsp. garlic powder

2 tsp. sea salt

––––––––––

2 racks baby back ribs

Directions

1. Preheat the oven to 325° F.

2. Dry rub: combine five-spice, brown sugar, onion powder, garlic powder, and sea salt. Use to coat ribs.

3. Arrange ribs on the Grill Pan. Cook in the oven for 1 ½ hours or until tender.

4. Serve ribs with your favorite side dishes.

Eric's Tip: Chinese five-spice is a blend of cinnamon, cloves, fennel, star anise, and Szechwan peppercorns. Some recipes might contain ginger or anise.

Lamb Loin Chops with Eric's Red Meat Rub

Ingredients

Eric's Red Meat Rub

2 tbsp. crushed sea salt

2 tbsp. brown sugar

2 tbsp. ground black coffee

1 tbsp. granulated garlic

1 tbsp. granulated onion

1 tbsp. cumin

1 tbsp. coriander

1 tbsp. ground black pepper

12 lamb loin chops

Directions

1. Distribute rub evenly over the lamb chops.

2. Grill the lamb on medium heat, 5-7 minutes on each side or to desired temperature.

3. Let rest 10 minutes before serving with your favorite side dishes.

Eric's Tip: Try using this with a nice thick tuna steak!

Eric's Surf & Turf

Ingredients

2 (10-oz.) rib eye steaks

2 (6-oz.) lobster tails

lemon wedges, for serving

Eric's Red Meat Rub

¼ cup sea salt

¼ cup brown sugar

¼ cup ground black coffee

2 tbsp. granulated garlic

3 tbsp. granulated onion

1 tbsp. cumin, ground

1 tbsp. coriander

1 tbsp. ground black pepper

Eric's Fish Rub

½ tsp. sea salt

½ tsp. onion powder

½ tsp. thyme

½ tsp. tarragon

½ tbsp. dried parsley

½ tbsp. dried chives

½ tsp. ground white pepper

½ tsp. dried lemon peel

½ tsp. celery seed

Directions

1. Cover steaks with red meat rub on each side.

2. Sprinkle lobster with fish rub.

3. Grill steaks and lobster until done.

4. Serve with lemon wedges and your favorite side dishes.

Eric's Tip: The whole thing about surf and turf is that you can use any cut of meat, fish or seafood. You can tailor it to your personal tastes and to what is fresh or available at the market.

Grilled Skirt Steak with Salsa Verde

SERVES 4

Ingredients

Marinade

2 limes, juiced

4 cloves garlic, peeled & chopped

1 tbsp. coriander, ground

10 sprigs cilantro, chopped

½ cup olive oil

1 tbsp. sea salt

1 tbsp. sriracha sauce

_____

2 skirt steaks (2 ½ lb.)

Salsa Verde

8 tomatillos, husked & rinsed

2 serrano peppers

½ small onion, peeled & chopped

1 clove garlic, peeled

8 sprigs fresh cilantro

1 tsp. sea salt

juice of ½ lime

Directions

1. Combine all marinade ingredients in a pan with steaks. Marinate in the refrigerator for 1-2 hours.

2. Grill the tomatillos, peppers, garlic, and onions until tender. Purée in a blender with remaining salsa ingredients. Set aside.

3. Remove steak from marinade. Pat dry with paper towels. Grill 5-7 minutes per side or to desired doneness.

4. Let rest 10 minutes before slicing. Serve steak warm with salsa verde.

Eric's Tip: For the best street tacos, add warmed corn tortillas, chopped red onion and crumbled queso fresco.

Hanger Steak & Green Peppercorn Butter

SERVES 4

Ingredients

2 lb. hanger steak

1 tbsp. sea salt

1 tbsp. course ground black peppercorns

¼ cup olive oil

**Bleu Cheese
Green Peppercorn Butter**

½ lb. butter

¼ cup Bleu cheese, crumbled

1 tbsp. green peppercorns, chopped

1 shallot, peeled & minced

½ tbsp. Dijon mustard

Directions

1. Rub the steak with sea salt, pepper, and olive oil.

2. With an electric mixer, blend butter ingredients until creamy.

3. Grill steaks to desired temperature.

4. Allow steaks to rest before slicing. Top with peppercorn butter immediately before serving.

Eric's Tip: Don't forget to slice the meat against the grain or you will risk a tough piece of steak.

Flank Steak with Balsamic Onion Dressing

SERVES 6

Ingredients

1 flank steak

1 tsp. sea salt

1 tsp. ground black pepper

2 tbsp. olive oil

Balsamic Onion Dressing

6 cipollini onions, peeled

¼ cup balsamic vinegar

½ cup extra virgin olive oil

1 sprig thyme, chopped

1 tsp. sea salt

½ tsp. ground black pepper

1 tsp. sugar

Directions

1. Rub flank steak with sea salt, pepper, and olive oil.

2. Mix dressing ingredients together.

3. Remove onions from dressing and grill until tender. Cut onions into quarters before returning to the dressing.

4. Grill the steaks to desired temperature.

5. Let steaks rest before slicing. Drizzle with dressing before serving with your favorite side dish.

Eric's Tip: If you can't find cipollini onions, you can substitute frozen pearl onions. Just make sure they're thawed and patted dry.

Grilled Filet with Porcini Compound Butter

Ingredients

Compound Butter

Step 1

¼ cup porcini mushrooms, dried

½ cup red wine

½ shallot, peeled & diced

Step 2

½ tsp. sea salt

½ tsp. black pepper, ground

2 sprigs tarragon, chopped

½ lb. butter, sweet, softened

½ tbsp. Dijon mustard

6 (8-oz.) beef tenderloin filets

1 tbsp. sea salt

½ tbsp. ground black pepper

Directions

1. In a saucepot, combine mushrooms, red wine, and shallot. Bring to a boil and reduce by ²/₃. Set aside to cool.

2. Combine sea salt, black pepper, tarragon, butter, and Dijon mustard in a bowl. Mix. Combine with mushroom mixture.

3. Season filets with sea salt and pepper. Grill 4-5 minutes per side or to desired temperature.

4. Top filets with butter before serving.

Eric's Tip: Mix this butter into rice, pasta, veggies or even make an awesome garlic bread with it. My favorite is to mash it into a baked potato.

Filet with Mushrooms & Shallots

SERVES 6

Ingredients

6 beef filets, 6 oz.

2 tbsp. olive oil

1 tbsp. sea salt

1 tbsp. ground black pepper

1 lb. cremini mushrooms

2 shallots, peeled & minced

2 tbsp. butter, soft

2 sprigs rosemary

Directions

1. Preheat the Griddle Pan on high heat for 4 minutes.

2. Rub the filets with olive oil, sea salt, and pepper.

3. Sear the filets on each side, about 5-7 minutes or to desired temperature. Plate filets and set aside.

4. Cook mushrooms and shallots on the Pan with butter and rosemary, 6-7 minutes.

5. Serve filets with mushrooms and shallots.

Griddle Recipe

Veggies

Shishito Peppers with Feta & Herbs

SERVES 4

Ingredients

½ lb. shishito peppers

½ cup extra virgin olive oil

4 cloves garlic, peeled & sliced

1 tsp. sea salt

½ tsp. hot red pepper flakes

½ cup feta cheese

1 sprig rosemary, chopped

2 sprigs thyme, chopped

Directions

1. In a bowl, combine peppers with olive oil, garlic, sea salt, and red pepper flakes.

2. Grill peppers with garlic on all sides to desired doneness. Reserve remaining olive oil.

3. Plate garlic and peppers. Sprinkle with remaining olive oil, from step 1, feta, and herbs.

4. Serve peppers alone or with your favorite protein. (I recommend the Skirt Steak.)

Eric's Tip: Don't be afraid of the shishito pepper. It's only a little hotter than a bell pepper, well below a jalapeño.

Lemony Asparagus with Basil & Oregano

SERVES 4

Ingredients

1 lb. asparagus

3 tbsp. extra virgin olive oil

1 tsp. sea salt

½ tsp. red pepper flakes

½ tsp. garlic powder, granulated

½ tsp. dried oregano

6 basil leaves, chopped

zest of ½ lemon

juice of ½ lemon

Directions

1. Toss asparagus with olive oil, sea salt, red pepper flakes, and garlic powder.

2. Grill on medium heat until tender.

3. Sprinkle asparagus with oregano, basil, lemon zest, and lemon juice immediately before serving.

Eric's Tip: If fresh asparagus isn't available, you can substitute fresh green beans or even baby bok choy.

Grilled Corn with Cilantro Aioli

SERVES 4

Ingredients

4 ears corn, shucked

Cilantro Aioli

1 cup mayonnaise

½ cup packed fresh cilantro

1 clove garlic, peeled

1 cup feta cheese

1 tbsp. sriracha, for serving

Directions

1. On high heat, grill the corn on all sides.

2. Cilantro aioli: in a blender, combine mayonnaise, cilantro, and garlic.

3. Brush the corn with aioli and roll in feta cheese.

4. Drizzle with sriracha before serving.

Eric's Tip: After grilling, slice into 2-inch sections then skewer the cobb for "lollipop" style appetizers.

Grilled Eggplant Parm

SERVES 6

Ingredients

12 eggplant slices, ½ inch rounds

2 cloves garlic, peeled & minced

½ cup olive oil

2 tbsp. red wine vinegar

1 tbsp. sea salt

½ tsp. ground black pepper

12 tomato slices

12 mozzarella slices

2 tbsp. Parmigiano-Reggiano cheese, grated

1 cup marinara sauce, heated

Directions

1. In a bowl, marinate the eggplant with garlic, olive oil, vinegar, sea salt, and pepper for one hour.

2. Drain the marinade from the eggplant. Grill on both sides.

3. Preheat the oven to 350° F.

4. Arrange eggplant onto the Grill Pan. Layer with tomato, mozzarella, and Parmigiano. Bake in the oven for 15 minutes.

5. Serve warm with marinara sauce.

Eric's Tip: I love adding grilled zucchini, yellow squash and portobello mushrooms for a Primavera Parmigiana.

Grilled Veggie Kabobs

Ingredients

1 red peppers, large dice

1 yellow pepper, large dice

1 zucchini, 1 inch rounds

1 yellow squash, 1 inch rounds

12 medium mushrooms

1 red onion, large dice

Marinade

¾ cup cider vinegar

2 tbsp. basil, chopped

2 tbsp. parsley, chopped

2 cloves garlic, peeled & minced

1 tbsp. sea salt

1 tsp. ground black pepper

Directions

1. Skewer the vegetables.

2. Marinade: in a bowl, combine vinegar, herbs, garlic, sea salt, and pepper. Pour over vegetable skewers. Marinate for 1 hour.

3. Drain the marinade from the kabobs. Arrange kabobs on the Grill Pan, rotating until vegetables are tender.

4. Serve with your favorite vegetable.

Eric's Tip: I always have a warm pita schmeared with hummus ready to wrap around the kabobs when they come hot off the Grill Pan.

190

Chipotle-Grilled Cauliflower Steaks

SERVES 4

Ingredients

1 large head cauliflower,
sliced into 1 inch thick steaks

Marinade

½ cup extra virgin olive oil

2 tbsp. rice wine vinegar

1 lime, juiced

2 cloves garlic, peeled & minced

Chipotle Rub

1 tbsp. sea salt

½ tbsp. ground black pepper

1 tbsp. chipotle powder

½ cup cilantro leaves, chopped,
to serve

Directions

1. In a pan, marinate the cauliflower with olive oil, vinegar, lime juice, and garlic for one hour.

2. Chipotle rub: in a separate bowl, combine sea salt, pepper, and chipotle powder.

3. Drain the marinade from the cauliflower. Sprinkle with chipotle rub.

4. On medium heat, grill the cauliflower on both sides.

5. Sprinkle cauliflower with cilantro before serving.

Eric's Tip: I'll swap the chipotle for curry powder to give this dish an exotic, Middle Eastern flair.

Grilled Asparagus & Feta

Ingredients

1 lb. asparagus, trimmed

¼ cup extra virgin olive oil

½ tsp. sea salt

½ tsp. black pepper, ground

juice of 1 lemon

½ cup feta, crumbled

¼ cup pine nuts, lightly toasted

1 tsp. dried oregano

Directions

1. Coat asparagus with olive oil. Season with salt and pepper.

2. Preheat the Grill Pan on medium heat. Grill asparagus until cooked.

3. Sprinkle asparagus with lemon juice, feta, pine nuts, and dried oregano before serving.

Eric's Tip: If fresh asparagus is not available, green beans can be substituted.

Zucchini Fritters

Ingredients

1 zucchini, shredded

⅓ cup flour

⅓ cup grated Parmesan cheese

2 eggs

¼ tsp. sea salt

½ tsp. ground black pepper

½ small onion, diced

1 clove garlic peeled & minced

3 tbsp. olive oil

Directions

1. In a bowl, combine all the ingredients except olive oil.

2. Preheat the Griddle Pan for 4 minutes on medium heat.

3. Coat the Pan with olive oil.

4. Drop heaping tablespoons of fritter batter onto the Pan.

5. Cook on both sides until golden.

Griddle Recipe

Banana Split Pizza

Grilled Cinnamon S'mores Toast

Salted Caramel
Peanut Butter Sundae

Grilled Doughnut Triple Decker
Ice Cream Sandwich

Grilled Banana Split Sundae

Grilled Peaches & Berries
Over Vanilla Ice Cream

Apple Pie Panini

Grilled Pear Crisp

Grilled Apple Pie

Grilled Pound Cake & Fruit

Grilled Fruit Skewers

Grilled Strawberry Shortcake

Grilled Pineapple Sundae

Brioche French Toast

Grilled Apple Bowls
& Vanilla Ice Cream

Sweet Potato Pancakes

Peanut Butter & Jelly Pancake

Banana Coconut Fritters

Chocolate Whoopie Pies

French Toast Sundae

Desserts

Banana Split Pizza

Ingredients

1 (8-oz.) thin crust pizza dough

¼ cup caramel sauce

2 bananas, sliced & grilled

8 strawberries, halved & grilled

2 tbsp. chocolate sauce

2 tbsp. raspberry sauce

¼ cup peanuts, chopped

Directions

1. Arrange pizza dough to fit onto the Grill Pan. Cook on both sides to desired doneness.

2. Spread caramel sauce over the pizza. Layer with bananas and strawberries.

3. Drizzle with chocolate and raspberry sauces. Top with peanuts.

4. Cut pizza into 8 slices. Serve alone or with your favorite ice cream.

Eric's Tip: Sprinkling toasted coconut or crumbled graham crackers will add extra flavor and crunch!

Grill Press
Accessory is required for this recipe.

SERVES 2

Ingredients

½ cup sugar

1 tbsp. cinnamon

4 slices bread

¼ cup margarine

15 baby marshmallows

1 (4.4-oz.) chocolate bar

Grilled Cinnamon S'mores Toast

Directions

1. Combine sugar and cinnamon in a bowl.

2. Spread margarine over one side of each slice of bread. Sprinkle with cinnamon and sugar mixture.

3. Arrange two slices of bread onto the Grill Pan, margarine side down. Cover each slice with marshmallows and half of the chocolate bar.

4. Top with remaining two slices of bread. Use **Grill Press** to cook on both sides, 3 minutes per side.

5. Serve alone or with a tall glass of milk!

Eric's Tip: As if this couldn't get any better, try a little peanut butter inside!

Salted Caramel Peanut Butter Sundae

MAKES 4

Ingredients

4 bananas, peeled & sliced into medallions

4 large scoops vanilla ice cream

½ cup creamy peanut butter

½ cup caramel sauce

¼ cup peanuts, chopped

pink sea salt, to sprinkle

Directions

1. Grill bananas on high heat.

2. Scoop ice cream into a serving bowl. Top with bananas, then peanut butter, caramel sauce, and chopped peanuts.

3. Sprinkle lightly with pink sea salt before serving.

Eric's Tip: Sprinkle the bananas with cinnamon and cayenne pepper before grilling for a little kick!

Grilled Doughnut Triple Decker Ice Cream Sandwich

SERVES 4

Ingredients

4 apple cider doughnuts, sliced in half

2 pears, halved, cored & sliced

4 cups vanilla ice cream

½ cup chocolate sauce

whipped cream, for serving

Directions

1. Arrange doughnut and pears halves on the Grill Pan. Cook to desired doneness.

2. Place the ice cream in a small baking pan and cover with plastic wrap. Press flat, about 2 inches thick, then place the pan into the freezer.

3. Cut frozen ice cream into 8 discs the same size as the doughnuts.

4. Place one doughnut half on each dish. Layer with sliced pears and ice cream. Top with a second doughnut half. Repeat to make it a triple decker

5. Drizzle with chocolate sauce and whipped cream before serving.

Eric's Tip: The key to this recipe is to use the best seasonal fruit. Local orchards and farm stands will keep the variety of this recipe endless!

Grilled Banana Split Sundae

Ingredients

Strawberry Sauce

8 oz. strawberries

2 tsp. sugar

Pineapple Sauce

8 oz. pineapple rounds

¼ cup light brown sugar

Sundae Basics

4 bananas, halved lengthwise

vanilla ice cream

chocolate ice cream

chocolate sauce

½ cup peanuts, chopped

whipped cream

Directions

1. Grill strawberries, pineapple, and banana halves to desired doneness. Set aside.

2. Strawberry sauce: in a small saucepan, combine the grilled strawberries with sugar. Cook until sugar is dissolved and strawberries are blended.

3. Pineapple sauce: in a separate saucepan, combine the grilled pineapples with light brown sugar. Cook until sugar is dissolved and pineapples are blended.

4. Assemble the sundae: line a dish with grilled bananas. Top with 3 scoops vanilla and / or chocolate ice cream and fruit sauces.

5. Sprinkle with peanuts. Top with chocolate sauce and whipped cream before serving.

Eric's Tip: I love using this grilled fruit sauce to flavor my margaritas!

Grilled Peaches & Berries Over Vanilla Ice Cream

SERVES 2

Ingredients

Simple Syrup

½ cup water

½ cup sugar

1 cinnamon stick

orange liqueur

---

2 peaches, halved & pitted

6 strawberries, halved

vanilla ice cream

Garnish

½ cup fresh blueberries

mint

Directions

1. Simple syrup: bring water, sugar, and cinnamon stick to a boil. Add orange liqueur.

2. Combine peaches and strawberries in a bowl with simple syrup. Soak for 1 hour at room temperature.

3. Place the Grill Pan on high heat. Grill strawberries and peaches until tender.

4. Top ice cream with grilled fruit. Garnish with blueberries and fresh mint immediately before serving.

Eric's Tip: I love combining flatbread, chocolate hazelnut spread, and grilled fruit for an amazing dessert pizza!

Apple Pie Panini

Ingredients

8 slices white bread

4 tbsp. butter, softened

2 granny smith apples, cored, halved & sliced thin

¼ cup brown sugar

1 tsp. cinnamon

½ cup cream cheese, softened

2 cups vanilla ice cream

Directions

1. Brush the bread on one side with butter.

2. In a bowl, combine the apples, brown sugar, and cinnamon. Mix.

3. Spread cream cheese thinly on the unbuttered side of the bread.

4. Assemble the paninis with the apple mixture and second slice of bread.

5. Grill on each side at medium heat until golden.

6. Cut paninis in half before serving with vanilla ice cream.

Eric's Tip: I love trying different cheeses with this recipe. Yellow cheddar and Brie are my two favorites!

Grilled Pear Crisp

Ingredients

2 pears, cored

Crisp Topping

¼ cup brown sugar

¼ cup flour

3 tbsp. butter

2 tbsp. walnuts

½ tsp. cinnamon

2 cups vanilla ice cream

4 tbsp. caramel sauce

Directions

1. Grill pears until tender. About 5 minutes per side.

2. Make crisp topping: combine brown sugar, flour, butter, walnuts, and cinnamon in a bowl.

3. Bake in the oven for 15 minutes at 400° F.

4. Place half a pear into each serving bowl. Immediately before serving, top with ½ cup vanilla ice cream, 2 tbsp. crisp topping, and 1 tbsp. caramel sauce.

Eric's Tip: Feel free to substitute any fruit that is ripe and in season such as local apples or peaches.

Grilled Apple Pie

SERVES 4

Ingredients

2 tbsp. butter

3 tbsp. brown sugar

3 apples, cored & sliced

2 sheets puff pastry

1 egg yolk

1 tbsp. milk

½ tsp. nutmeg

1 tsp. cinnamon

Directions

1. Melt butter and brown sugar in a saucepot. Add apples. Cook, tossing occasionally, for 5 minutes or until tender. Set aside to cool.

2. Arrange 1 sheet puff pastry onto an unheated Grill Pan.

3. In a bowl, mix egg yolk and milk. Use to brush edges of puff pastry.

4. Toss apples with nutmeg and cinnamon.

5. Arrange apple slices on top of the puff pastry. Leave one inch of pastry untouched on all sides.

6. Preheat the oven to 400° F.

7. Top apples with second sheet of puff pastry. Seal on all sides.

8. Grill on medium-low heat for about 10 minutes.

9. Brush the top with egg and milk mixture. Bake in the oven for 15 minutes or until golden.

10. Allow pie to cool. Cut and serve with vanilla ice cream and caramel sauce.

Eric's Tip: If they are in season, sprinkle some fresh berries on top of the apples before placing the top puff pastry.

Grilled Pound Cake & Fruit

SERVES 6

Ingredients

6 slices pound cake

3 peaches, sliced & pitted

3 bananas, peeled & sliced

24 strawberries, large

½ cup simple syrup

¼ cup raspberry sauce

1 cup whipped cream

6 mint leaves, for garnish

Directions

1. Arrange the pound cake, peaches, bananas, and strawberries on the Grill Pan. Cook on both sides to desired doneness.

2. Toss the fruit with simple syrup. Set aside.

3. Plate the pound cake with grilled fruit.

4. Top with raspberry sauce and whipped cream. Garnish with mint leaves immediately before serving.

Eric's Tip: Another delicious variation on this recipe is to slice a corn muffin in half and grill. The fruit and cream complement the corn's sweetness.

Grilled Fruit Skewers

SERVES 6

Ingredients

8 strawberries, large

2 peaches, sliced thick

1 pear, sliced thick

1 cup pineapple, cubed

1 banana, sliced thick

Chocolate Dipping Sauce

1 cup heavy cream

1 cup semi-sweet chocolate chips

½ tsp. vanilla extract

Directions

1. Skewer the cut fruit. Grill to desired doneness.

2. Dipping sauce: in a saucepot, bring the heavy cream to a boil. Add the chocolate chips and remove from heat.

3. Stir until creamy, then add vanilla.

4. Serve grilled fruit with chocolate dipping sauce.

Eric's Tip: Feel free to choose any chocolate you like. Dark and white work well with this recipe.

Grilled Strawberry Shortcake

SERVES 6

Ingredients

1 angel food cake, sliced into wedges

½ stick butter

1 lb. strawberries, cut in half

zest of 1 lemon

juice of ½ lemon

1 tbsp. sugar

1 ½ cup heavy cream

¼ cup confectioners' sugar, to whip cream

1 tsp. vanilla extract

Directions

1. Brush the cake wedges with butter. Grill to desired doneness.

2. Grill the strawberries. Let cool before tossing with lemon zest, lemon juice, and 1 tbsp. sugar.

3. Whip the cream with ¼ cup confectioners' sugar and vanilla.

4. Top cake wedges with strawberries and whipped cream immediately before serving.

Eric's Tip: I've diced the grilled angel food cake and turned this into an amazing layered trifle when making dessert for a large group!

Grilled Pineapple Sundae

SERVES 2

Ingredients

¼ pineapple, peeled & sliced

2 cups vanilla ice cream

¼ cup whipped cream

¼ cup sliced almonds

Directions

1. Grill the pineapple until tender. Let cool before chopping.

2. Scoop ice cream into 2 serving dishes. Immediately before serving, top with pineapple, whipped cream, and sliced almonds.

Eric's Tip: You can also make an awesome dessert "salsa" by adding chopped strawberries and fresh mint.

Brioche French Toast

Ingredients

10 eggs

¾ cup half and half

2 tsp. cinnamon

1 tsp. almond extract

¼ cup maple syrup, to serve

1 loaf brioche bread, sliced

1 stick butter

Directions

1. In a bowl beat the eggs. Mix in half and half, cinnamon, and almond extract.

2. Soak bread in the egg batter for 5 minutes.

3. Preheat the Griddle Pan on medium heat, 3-4 minutes.

4. Melt 2 tbsp. butter onto the Pan. Cook the French toast to desired doneness. Repeat until all are cooked.

5. Serve with maple syrup and butter.

Griddle Recipe

Grilled Apple Bowls & Vanilla Ice Cream

SERVES 4

Ingredients

Simple Syrup

1 cup sugar

1 cup water

1 cinnamon stick

---

2 apples, large

2 cups vanilla ice cream

½ cup caramel sauce

½ cup pecans, chopped

Directions

1. Simple syrup: in a saucepan, bring the sugar, water, and cinnamon stick to a boil. Set aside.

2. Cut the apples in half and core with a melon baller. Add to the hot simple syrup.

3. Arrange apples on the Grill Pan, cut side down. Cook for 3 minutes. Turn over and continue grilling until tender. Baste with simple syrup.

4. Top the apples with ice cream, caramel sauce, and chopped pecans immediately before serving.

Eric's Tip: These apples can also be made in advance. After grilling, cool in the refrigerator. When you are ready to serve, warm up in the microwave.

Sweet Potato Pancakes

SERVES 2

Ingredients

Wet

¾ cup sweet potato, cooked & pureed

2 eggs

1 cup buttermilk

3 tbsp. butter, melted, for batter

Dry

1 cup flour

2 tsp. baking powder

½ tsp. salt

½ tsp. cinnamon

¼ tsp. nutmeg

1 tbsp. brown sugar

2 tbsp. butter, for cooking

To Serve

walnut or pecan syrup

bananas

Directions

1. Mix the wet ingredients together and set aside.

2. In a bowl, mix all dry ingredients together.

3. Combine wet ingredients and dry ingredients.

4. Preheat Griddle Pan on medium heat and melt 2 tbsp. butter.

5. Cook pancakes to desired doneness.

6. Serve with walnut or pecan syrup and bananas.

Griddle Recipe

Peanut Butter & Jelly Pancake

Ingredients

Pancakes

2 eggs

1 ½ cups whole milk

½ cup smooth peanut butter

1 ¼ cups pancake mix

Peanut Butter Cream

½ cup smooth peanut butter

1 (8-oz.) container whipped topping

Grape Syrup

¼ cup grape jelly

½ cup maple syrup

Directions

1. Preheat the Griddle Pan over medium heat.

2. Make pancake batter: whisk together the egg and milk.

3. Add the peanut butter and whisk until smooth.

4. Stir in the pancake mix.

5. Peanut butter cream: whisk together the peanut butter and whipped topping.

6. Grape syrup: combine the jelly and syrup. Microwave until melted, about 20 seconds. Stir to combine.

7. Ladle a half cup of the pancake batter onto the Pan. Cook until golden brown, about 2 minutes per side.

8. Continue until all batter is used up.

9. Stack the pancakes, spreading a smear of the peanut butter cream between each pancake.

10. Drizzle with the grape syrup before serving.

Griddle Recipe

Banana Coconut Fritters

Ingredients

2 bananas, mashed

⅓ cup flour

½ tsp. cinnamon

2 eggs

½ cup shredded coconut

½ tsp. baking powder

1 tbsp. brown sugar

1 tbsp. milk

3 tbsp. canola oil

Directions

1. Combine all ingredients except oil in a bowl.

2. Preheat Griddle Pan for 4 minutes on medium heat.

3. Coat the Pan with canola oil.

4. Drop heaping tablespoons of fritter batter onto the Pan.

5. Cook until golden on each side before serving.

Griddle Recipe

Chocolate Whoopie Pies

MAKES 8

Ingredients

⅓ cup cocoa powder

1 ½ cup flour

1 tsp. baking soda

½ tsp. salt

¾ cup buttermilk

¾ cup butter

¾ cup brown sugar

1 egg

½ tsp. vanilla extract

Marshmallow Cream Filling

¾ stick butter

1 cup confectioners' sugar

1 ⅔ cups marshmallow cream

1 tsp. vanilla extract

Directions

1. Preheat the oven to 350° F.

2. In a bowl, sift the cocoa powder, flour, baking soda, and salt.

3. In an electric mixer, cream the buttermilk, butter, and brown sugar together.

4. Add the egg and vanilla. Mix until incorporated.

5. Slowly add the flour mixture to the creamed ingredients. Blend.

6. Make first batch of cake halves: arrange eight ¼ cup scoops of cake mix onto the Griddle Pan. Bake 12-15 minutes or until done.

7. Repeat step 6 to make second batch of cake halves.

8. In the mixer, cream the butter and confectioners' sugar together until creamy. Add the marshmallow and vanilla.

9. Place the marshmallow cream in a piping bag and fill the whoopie pies.

Griddle Recipe

French Toast Sundae

Ingredients

2 cups half and half

6 eggs

1 tsp. vanilla extract

1 tsp. salt

2 tbsp. cinnamon

1 loaf challah bread, sliced into 1" pieces

2 tbsp. butter, melted

To Serve

vanilla ice cream

chopped walnuts

maple syrup

whipped cream

Directions

1. Preheat the Griddle Pan over medium heat.

2. In a large bowl, combine the half and half, eggs, vanilla, salt, and cinnamon. Whisk to combine.

3. Quickly submerge challah slices fully into the egg mixture.

4. Brush the Pan with butter. Place the challah onto the Pan. Cook until golden brown, about 2-3 minutes per side.

5. To serve, cut two pieces of French toast in half and arrange in a dish or bowl.

6. Top with vanilla ice cream and some chopped walnuts.

7. Drizzle with maple syrup and garnish with whipped cream before serving.

Griddle Recipe

Index